Sowing and Reaping

Sowing and Reaping

by Dwight Lyman Moody

'Whatsoever a man soweth, that shall he also reap.'
Gal. vi: 7.

CONTENTS.

Chap.

SOWING AND REAPING.

CHAPTER I.

"Be not deceived; God is not mocked: for whatsoever a man soweth, that shall he also reap. For he that soweth to his flesh shall of the flesh reap corruption; but he that soweth to the Spirit shall of the Spirit reap life everlasting." Galatians vi: 7, 8.

I think this passage contains truths that no infidel or sceptic will dare to deny. There are some passages in the Word of God that need no other proof than that which we can easily find in our daily experience. This is one of them. If the Bible were to be blotted out of existence, the words I have quoted would be abundantly verified by what is constantly happening around us. We have only to take up the daily papers to see them being fulfilled before our eyes.

I remember giving out this text once when a man stood right up in the audience and said:

"I don't believe it."

I said, "My friend, that doesn't change the fact. Truth is truth whether you believe it or not, and a lie is a lie whether you believe it or not."

He didn't want to believe it. When the meeting broke up, an officer was at the door to arrest him. He was tried and sent to the penitentiary for twelve months for stealing. I really believe that when he got into his cell, he believed that he had to reap what he sowed.

We might as well try to blot the sun out of the heavens as to blot this truth out of the Word of God. It is heaven's eternal decree. The law has been enforced for six thousand years. Did not God make Adam reap even before he left Eden? Had not Cain to reap outside of Eden? A king on the throne, like David, or a priest behind the altar, like Eli; priest and prophet, preacher and hearer, every man must reap what he sows. I believed it ten years ago, but I believe it a hundred times more to-day.

My text applies to the individual, whether he be saint or sinner or hypocrite who thinks he is a saint; it applies to the family; it applies to society; it applies to nations. I say the law that the result of actions must be reaped is *as true for nations as for individuals;*

4

indeed, some one has said that as nations have no future existence, the present world is the only place to punish them as nations. See how God has dealt with them. See if they have not reaped what they sowed. Take Amalek: "Remember what Amalek did unto thee by the way, when ye were come forth out of Egypt; how he met thee, by the way, and smote the hindmost of thee, even all that were feeble behind thee, when thou wast faint and weary; and he feared not God." What was to be the result of this attack? Was it to go unpunished? God ordained that Amalek should reap as they sowed, and the nation was all but wiped out of existence under King Saul.

What has become of the monarchies and empires of the world? What brought ruin on Babylon? Her king and people would not obey God, and ruin came upon them. What has become of Greece and all her power? She once ruled the world. What has become of Rome and all her greatness? When their cup of iniquity was full, it was dashed to the ground. What has become of the Jews? They rejected salvation, persecuted God's messengers, and crucified their Redeemer; and we find that eleven hundred thousand of them perished at one time. Look at the history of this country. With an open Bible, our forefathers planted slavery; but judgment came at last. There was not a family North or South that had not to mourn over some one taken from them. Take the case of France. It is said that a century ago men were spending millions every year in France in the publication and distribution of infidel literature. What has been the harvest? Has France not reaped? Mark the result: "The Bible was suppressed. God was denied. Hell broke loose. Half the children born in Paris were bastards. More than a million of persons were beheaded, shot, drowned, outraged, and done to death between September, 1792, and December, 1795. Since that time France has had thirteen revolutions in eighty years; and in the republic there has been an overturn on an average once in nine months. One-third of the births in Paris are illegitimate; ten thousand new-born infants have been fished out at the outlet of the city sewers in a single year; the native population of France is decreasing; the percentage of suicides is greater in Paris than in any city in Christendom; and since the French Revolution there have been enough French men and women slaughtered in the streets of Paris in the various insurrections, to average more than two thousand five hundred each year!"

The principle was not new in Scripture or in history when Paul enunciated it in his letter to the Galatians. Paul clothes it in language derived from the farm, but in other dress the Law of Sowing and Reaping may be seen in the Law of Cause and Effect, the Law of Retribution or Retaliation, the Law of Compensation. It is not to my purpose to enter now into a philosophical discussion of the law as it appears under any of these names. We see that it exists. It is beyond reasonable dispute. Whatever else sceptics may carp at and criticise in the Bible, they must acknowledge the truth of this. It does not depend upon revelation for its support; philosophers are agreed upon it as much as they are agreed upon any thing.

The Supremacy of Law.

The objection may be made, however, that while its application may be admitted in the physical world, it is not so certain in the spiritual sphere. It is just here that modern research steps in. The laws of the spiritual world have been largely identified as the same laws that exist in the natural world. Indeed, it is claimed that the spiritual existed first, that the natural came after, and that when God proceeded to frame the universe, He went upon lines already laid down. In short, that God projected the higher laws downward, so that the natural world became "an incarnation, a visible representation, a working model of the supernatural." "In the spiritual world the same wheels work—without the iron."

Our whole life is thus bounded and governed by laws ordained and established by God, and that a man reaps what he sows is a law that can be easily observed and verified, whether we regard sowing to the flesh or sowing to the Spirit. The evil harvest of sin and the good harvest of righteousness are as sure to follow the sowing as the harvest of wheat and barley. "Life is not *casual*, but *causal*."

We shall see, as we proceed, that *the working of the law is evident in the earliest periods of Bible history*. Job's three friends reasoned that he must be a great sinner, because they took it for granted that the calamities that overtook him must be the results of his wickedness. "Remember, I pray thee," said one of them, "who ever perished, being innocent? or where were the righteous cut off?

Even as I have seen, they that plough iniquity, and sow wickedness, reap the same."

In the book of Proverbs we find it written: "The wicked worketh a deceitful work: but to him that soweth righteousness shall be a sure reward." And again: "He that soweth iniquity shall reap vanity."

In Isaiah we find these words: "Say ye to the righteous that it shall be well with him; for they shall eat the fruit of their doings. Woe unto the wicked! it shall be ill with him: for the reward of his hands shall be given him."

Hosea prophesied regarding Israel: "They have sown the wind, and they shall reap the whirlwind." "Sow to yourselves in righteousness," he advised them, "reap in mercy."

Teaching from Analogy.

The Bible is full of analogies drawn from nature. When Christ was on earth, it was His favorite mode of teaching to convey heavenly truths in earthly dress. "Truths came forth from His lips," wrote one, "not stated simply on authority, but based on the analogy of the universe. His human mind, in perfect harmony with the Divine mind with which it was united, discerned the connection of things, and read the eternal will in the simplest laws of nature. For instance, if it were a question whether God would give His Spirit to them that asked, it was not replied to by a truth revealed on His *authority:* the answer was derived from facts lying open to all men's observation. 'Behold the fowls of the air'; 'behold the lilies of the field'—learn from them the answer to your question. A principle was there. God supplies the wants He has created. He feeds the ravens—He clothes the lilies—He will feed with His Spirit the craving spirits of His children."

This is the style of teaching that Paul adopts in the text. He takes the simple process of sowing and reaping, a process familiar to all, and reads in it a deeply spiritual and moral meaning. It is as if he said that every man as he journeys through life is scattering seed at every step. The seed consists of his thoughts, his words, his actions. They pass from him, and by and by (it may be sooner or later), they spring up and bear fruit, and the reaping time comes.

Life a Seed-Time.

The analogy contains some solemn lessons. Life is to be regarded as a seed-time. Every one has his field to sow, to cultivate, and finally, to reap. By our habits, by our intercourse with friends and companions, by exposing ourselves to good or bad influences, we are cultivating the seed for the coming harvest. We cannot see the seed as it grows and develops, but time will reveal it.

Just as the full-grown harvest is potentially contained in the seed, so the full results of sin or holiness are potentially contained in the sinful or holy deed. "When lust hath conceived, it bringeth forth sin, and sin, when it is finished, bringeth forth death."

Just as we cannot reap a good harvest unless we have sown good seed, so we cannot reap eternal life unless we have sown to the Spirit. Weeds are easy to grow. They grow without the planting. And sin springs up naturally in the human heart. Ever since our first parents broke away from God, the human heart has of itself been thoroughly vile, and all its fruits have been evil. "The heart of the sons of men is fully set in them to do evil." Do you doubt it? If you do, ask yourself what would become of a child if it was left to itself—no training, no guidance, no education. In spite of all that is done for children, the evil too often gets the upper hand. The good seed must be planted and cared for, often with toil and trouble: but the harvest will be sure.

Do we desire the love of our fellows in our seasons of trial? Then we must love them when they need its cheering influence most. Do we long for sympathy in our sorrow and pain? Then we shall have it if we have also wept with those who weep. Are we hoping to reap eternal life? Then we must not sow to the flesh, or we shall reap corruption, but to the Spirit, then the promise is that we shall reap its immortal fruits.

Dr. Chalmers has drawn attention to *the difference between the act of sowing and the act of reaping.* "Let it be observed," he says, "that the act of indulging in the desires of the flesh is one thing and the act of providing for the indulgence of them is another. When a man, on the impulse of sudden provocation, wreaks his resentful feelings upon the neighbor who has offended him, he is not at that time preparing for the indulgence of a carnal feeling, but actually indulging it. He is not at that time sowing, but reaping (such as it is) a harvest of gratification. This distinction may serve to assist our judgment in estimating the ungodliness of certain characters. The rambling voluptuary who is carried along by every impulse, and all whose powers of mental discipline are so enfeebled that he has become the slave of every propensity, lives in the perpetual harvest of criminal gratification. A daughter whose sole delight is in her rapid transitions from one scene of expensive brilliancy to another, who dissipates every care and fills every hour among the frivolities and fascinations of her volatile society,—she leads a life than which nothing can be imagined more opposite to a life of preparation for the coming judgment or the coming eternity. Yet she *reaps* rather than *sows*. It lies with another to gather the money which purchaseth all things, and with her to taste the fruits of the purchase. *It is the father who sows.* It is he who sits in busy and brooding anxiety over his speculations, wrinkled, perhaps, by care, and sobered by years into an utter distaste for the splendors and insignificancies of fashionable life." The father sows, and he reaps in his daughter's life.

"Painting for Eternity."

A famous painter was well known for the careful manner in which he went about his work. When some one asked him why he took such pains, he replied:

"Because I am painting for eternity."

It is a solemn thing to think that *the future will be the harvest of the present*—that my condition in my dying hour may depend upon my actions to-day! Belief in a future life and in a coming judgment magnifies the importance of the present. Eternal issues depend upon it. The opportunity for sowing will not last forever; it is slipping through our fingers moment by moment; and the future can only reveal the harvest of the seed sown now.

A sculptor once showed a visitor his studio. It was full of statues of gods. One was very curious. The face was concealed by being covered with hair, and there were wings on each foot.

"What is his name?" said the visitor.

"Opportunity," was the reply.

"Why is his face hidden?"

"Because men seldom know him when he comes to them."

"Why has he wings on his feet?"

"Because he is soon gone, and once gone can never be overtaken."

It becomes us, then, to make the most of the opportunities God has given us. It depends a good deal on ourselves what our future shall be. We can sow for a good harvest, or we can do like the Sioux Indians, who once, when the United States Commissioner of Indian Affairs sent them a supply of grain for sowing, ate it up. Men are constantly sacrificing their eternal future to the passing enjoyment of the present moment; they fail or neglect to recognize the dependence of the future upon the present.

Nothing Trifling.

From this we may learn that there is no such thing as a trifle on earth. When we realize that every thought and word and act has an eternal influence, and will come back to us in the same way as the seed returns in the harvest, we must perceive their responsibility, however trifling they may seem. We are apt to overlook the results that hinge on small things. The law of gravitation was suggested by the fall of an apple. It is said that some years ago a Harvard professor brought some gypsy-moths to this country in the hope that they could with advantage be crossed with silkworms. The moths accidentally got away, and multiplied so enormously that the Commonwealth of Massachusetts has had to spend hundreds of thousands of dollars trying to exterminate them.

When H. M. Stanley was pressing his way through the forests of Darkest Africa, the most formidable foes that he encountered, those that caused most loss of life to his caravan and came the nearest to entirely defeating his expedition, were the little Wambutti dwarfs. So annoying were they that very slow progress could be made through their dwelling places.

These little men had only little bows and little arrows that looked like children's playthings, but upon these tiny arrows there was a small drop of poison which would kill an elephant or a man as quickly and as surely as a Winchester rifle. Their defense was by means of poison and traps. They would steal through the darkness of the forest and, waiting in ambush, let fly their deadly arrows before they could be discovered. They dug ditches and carefully covered them over with leaves. They fixed spikes in the ground and tipped them with the most deadly poison, and then covered them. Into these ditches and on these spikes man and beast would fall or step to their death.

A lady once writing to a young man in the navy who was almost a stranger, thought "Shall I close this as anybody would, or shall I say a word for my Master?" and, lifting up her heart for a moment, she wrote, telling him that his constant change of scene and place was an apt illustration of the word, "*Here we have no continuing city*," and asked if he could say: "I seek one to come." Tremblingly she folded it and sent it off.

Back came the answer. "Thank you so much for those kind words! I am an orphan, and no one has spoken to me like that since my mother died, long years ago." The arrow shot at venture hit home, and the young man shortly after rejoiced in the fulness of the blessing of the gospel of peace.

An obscure man preached one Sunday to a few persons in a Methodist chapel in the South of England. A boy of fifteen years of age was in the audience, driven into the chapel by a snowstorm. The man took as his text the words, "Look unto me and be ye saved," and as he stumbled along as best he could, the light of heaven flashed into that boy's heart. He went out of the chapel saved, and soon became known as C. H. Spurgeon, the boy-preacher.

The parsonage at Epworth, England, caught fire one night, and all the inmates were rescued except one son. The boy came to a window, and was brought safely to the ground by two farm-hands, one standing on the shoulder of the other. The boy was John Wesley. If you would realize the responsibility of that incident, if you would measure the consequences of that rescue, ask the millions of Methodists who look back to John Wesley as the founder of their denomination.

BE NOT DECEIVED; GOD IS NOT MOCKED.

"*Let no man deceive you.*"—Eph. v: 6.

"*As one man mocketh another, do ye so mock Him?*"—Job xiii: 9.

CHAPTER II.

Be Not Deceived: God Is Not Mocked.

We have all lived long enough to know what it is to be deceived. We have been deceived by our friends, by our enemies, our neighbors, our relatives. Ungodly companions have deceived us.

At every turn of life we have been imposed upon in one way or another.

False teachers have crossed our path, and under pretence of doing us good, have poisoned our mind with error. They have held out hopes to us that have proved false; apples of Sodom, fair without, but full of ashes within. They have told us that there is no God, no future life, no judgment to come; or they have said that all men will be saved, that there is ample time to repent, that we may be saved by doing the best we can.

Sin has deceived us. Every sinner is under a delusion. Sin meets him smilingly, and holds out to him pleasures and delights that are not pure and lasting.

During our meetings in Boston a young man came into the Tabernacle. He looked around, and he thought to himself the people that came there were great fools—those who had business, and comfortable homes, and good clothes. He had nothing in the world—he was a tramp, and went in there to keep himself warm. But to think that people who had homes would come and spend their time in listening to such stuff as I preached was more than he could understand.

One night after he had been coming there for two weeks, I happened to point right down where he was sitting, and I said, "Young man, be not deceived!" God used that as an arrow. He began to think about himself. His mind went back to the time when he had a good situation in Boston; when he was a young man getting a good salary; when he was in good society, and had a great many friends.

Then he looked at his present condition. His friends were all gone, his clothes were gone, his money was gone; and there he was, an outcast in that city. He said to himself, "I have been deceived," and that very hour God waked him. He wanted to get friends to pray for him; but as he was not able to buy a piece of paper, or pay for a postage stamp, he got an old piece of soiled paper, stood up in the street, and wrote a request to be read in the Tabernacle, that if God would save a poor, lost man like him, he wanted to be saved. That prayer was answered. As in the case of Nebuchadnezzar, his friends gathered around him again, and the Lord restored him to position and to society. His eyes were opened to see how he had been deceived.

12

Satan.

How many men all over the world are being deceived by the god of this world! It has been asserted that during the late Franco-German war, German drummers and trumpeters used to give the French beats and calls in order to deceive their enemies. The command to "halt," or "cease firing," was often given by the Germans, it has been said, and the French soldiers were thus placed in positions where they could be shot down like cattle.

Satan is the arch-enemy of our souls, and he has often blinded our reason and deceived our conscience by his falsehoods. He has often come as an angel of light, concealing his hideousness under a borrowed cloak. He says to a young man: "Sow your wild oats. Time enough to be religious when you grow old." The young man yields himself to a life of extravagance and excess, under the false hope that he will obtain solid satisfaction; and it is well if he awakens to the deception before his appetites become tyrants, dragging him down into depths of want and woe. Satan promises great things to his victims in the indulgence of their lusts, but they never realize the promises. The promised pleasure turns out to be pain, the promised heaven a hell.

Beware lest Satan deceive you as he deceived Eve in the beginning. "There is no truth in him. When he speaketh a lie, he speaketh of his own, for he is a liar, and the father of it."

Our Heart.

But we have been deceived by our own heart most of all. Who has not proved the truth of the Scripture: "The heart is deceitful above all things and desperately wicked; who can know it?" "How many times we have said that we never would do a certain thing again, and then have done it within twenty-four hours! A man may think he has fathomed its depths, but he finds there are further depths he has not reached. What gross self-deception is due to it! "He that trusteth in his own heart is a fool," said Solomon. Luther once said he feared his own heart more than the Pope and all the cardinals.

Many a weeping wife has come to me about her husband, saying: "He is good at heart." The truth is—that is the worst spot in him. If the heart was good, all else would be right. Out of the heart are the issues of life. Christ said: "From within, out of the heart of men, proceed evil thoughts, adulteries, fornications, murders, thefts, covetousness, wickedness, deceit, lasciviousness, an evil eye, blasphemy, pride, foolishness." That is Christ's own statement regarding the unregenerate heart.

Some years ago a remarkable picture was exhibited in London. As you looked at it from a distance, you seemed to see a monk engaged in prayer, his hands clasped, his head bowed. As you came nearer, however, and examined the painting more closely, you saw that in reality he was squeezing a lemon into a punchbowl!

What a picture that is of the human heart! Superficially examined, it is thought to be the seat of all that is good and noble and pleasing in a man; whereas in reality, until regenerated by the Holy Ghost, it is the seat of all corruption. "This is the condemnation, that light is come into the world, and men *loved darkness rather than light.*"

A Jewish rabbi once asked his scholars what was the best thing a man could have in order to keep him in the straight path. One said *a good disposition;* another, *a good companion;* another said *wisdom* was the best thing he could desire. At last a scholar replied that he thought *a good heart* was best of all.

"True," said the rabbi, "you have comprehended all that the others have said. For he that hath a good heart will be of a good disposition, and a good companion, and a wise man. Let every one, therefore, cultivate a sincerity and uprightness of heart at all times, and it will save him an abundance of sorrow." We need to make the prayer of David—"Create in me a clean heart, O God, and renew a right spirit within me!"

God Is Not Mocked.

Bear in mind, the God of the Bible has never deceived anyone, and never can, and never will; that is the difference between the God of the Bible and the god of this world. He beholds the ways of men; He looks into their hearts; He knows their secret ways; they need not tell Him or try to conceal anything from Him.

However successfully we may deceive or be deceived by ourselves or others, we cannot deceive Him. Adam and Eve tried it in Eden when they hid themselves from the presence of Jehovah amongst the trees of the garden. Saul tried it when he spared the best of the sheep and oxen of the Amalekites under the pretence of sacrificing them to God. Ananias and Sapphira tried it when they kept back part of the price of the land they sold. "Why hath Satan filled thine heart to lie unto (deceive) the Holy Ghost? * * * Thou hast not lied unto men, but unto God."

Men try it every day. They have got it into their heads that God can be mocked. Because they can deceive their pastor, and their employer, and their friends, they think they can deceive God. They put on false appearances, they use empty words, they perform unreal service, they make idle excuses, they indulge in all kinds of hypocrisy. But it is of no avail. God cannot be imposed upon. He sees the corruption inside the whited sepulchre.

Warning to Christians.

It is worth noticing that this warning was given by Paul to Christian men—converts in the Galatian church. After all, a man is not all the time deceived about the grosser sins. The drunkard realizes in his sober moments what must be the end of a course of intemperance. Loss of self-respect and of the esteem of friends, the marks he soon begins to bear in his body—unsteady hands and discolored features—these things are the quick harvest of drunkenness, and may easily be detected as they ripen. The licentious man, also, reaps the early fruit of his sin in diseases of the body, which are often effective warnings against continuing in such a dangerous path. But with "respectable" sins it is different. A man may be sowing for years, and not even realize it himself.

You remember that in the parable of the sower some seeds fell among thorns, and the thorns sprung up and choked them. Our Master, expounding this parable, said: "He that received seed among the thorns is he that heareth the word: but *the care of this world and the deceitfulness of riches* choke the word, and he becometh unfruitful." Who would have expected this result of the world or of riches? But it has been said that Christ never spoke of riches except in words of warning. We are not apt to regard them in that light to-day. Men are trampling each other down in the pursuit of wealth. "Be not deceived." He who sets his heart upon money is sowing to the flesh, and shall of the flesh reap corruption. "Adversity hath slain her thousands, but prosperity her tens of thousands."

"What is the value of this estate?" said a gentleman to another, as they passed a fine mansion surrounded by fair and fertile fields.

15

"I don't know what it is valued at; I know what it cost its late possessor."

"How much?"

"His soul."

An English clergyman was called to the death-bed of a wealthy parishioner. Kneeling beside the dying man the pastor asked him to take his hand as he prayed for his upholding in that solemn hour, but he declined to give it. After the end had come, and they turned down the coverlet, the rigid hands were found holding the safe-key in their death-grip. Heart and hand, to the last, clinging to his possessions, but he could not take them with him.

A man may be proud, and his very sin reckoned a virtue. Hear what the Word of God says: "Haughtiness of eyes and a proud heart is sin"; "every one that is proud in heart is an abomination to the Lord."

These are the mistakes men make. They are leading respectable lives, and they think that all is well. They do not recognize the taint of corruption upon many of the most cherished objects of their hearts. Christian professors, most of all, need to beware lest they are being deceived.

Neglect.

How watchful men should be of their thoughts, their practices, their feelings! The reason of deception is, for the most part, neglect. Men do not stop to examine themselves, to lay their hearts and minds bare as in the sight of God, and judge themselves by His most holy will. A man need not shoot himself in order to commit suicide: he need only neglect the proper means of sustenance, and he will soon die. Where an enemy is strong and aggressive, an army is doomed to sure defeat and capture unless a sharp look-out is kept, every man wide awake at his post of duty.

It has been noticed that there are more accidents in Switzerland in fine seasons than in stormy ones. People are apt to undertake expeditions that they would not take under less favorable conditions, and they are less careful in their conduct. And so it is that moral and spiritual disaster usually overtakes men when they are off their guard, careless against temptation. They become proud and self-reliant in seasons of prosperity, whereas adversity drives them to the living God for guidance and comfort.

Dr. Johnson once said that it is more from carelessness regarding the truth than from intentional lying that there is so much falsehood in the world.

Hence the necessity of continual watchfulness. The Persians had an annual festival when they slew all the serpents and venomous creatures they could find; but they allowed them to swarm as fast and freely as ever until the festival came round once more. It was poor policy. Sins, like serpents, breed quickly, and need to be constantly watched.

And we ought to watch on every side. Many a man has fallen at the very point where he thought he was safest. The meekness of Moses has passed into a proverb. Yet he lost the Promised Land, because he allowed the children of Israel to provoke him, and "he spake unadvisedly with his lips." Peter was the most zealous and defiant of the disciples, bold and outspoken; yet he degenerated for a short time into a lying, swearing, sneaking coward, afraid of a maid.

There is an old fable that a doe that had but one eye used to graze near the sea; and in order to be safe, she kept her blind eye toward the water, from which side she expected no danger, while with the good eye she watched the country. Some men, perceiving this, took a boat and came upon her from the sea and shot her. With her dying breath, she said:

"Oh! hard fate! that I should receive my death-wound from that side whence I expected no harm, and be safe in the part where I looked for most danger."

Let danger and need drive you closer to God. He never slumbers or sleeps, and in His keeping you will be safe. Seize hold of Him in prayer. "Watch and pray."

Christianity Not Responsible.

Christianity is not responsible for the deception that exists among its professing disciples. The illustration has been used before that you might just as reasonably hold the Cunard company responsible for the suicide of a passenger who jumps overboard one of their vessels at sea. Had the person remained on the vessel, he would have been safe; and had the disciple remained true to his principles, he would never have turned out a hypocrite. Was anybody ever more severe in denouncing hypocrisy than Christ? Do you want to know the reason why, every now and then, the church is scandalized by the exposure of some leading church member or Sabbath school superintendent? It is not his Christianity, but his lack of it. Some secret sin has been eating at the heart of the tree, and in a critical moment it is blown down and its rottenness revealed.

The Deception Can Not Last Forever.

It is impossible for the deception to last forever. Lincoln had a saying that you may be able to deceive all the people some of the time, and some of the people all of the time, but you will not be able to deceive all the people all of the time. Death will uncover the deception, if it has not been detected sooner; and the unfortunate victim will stand, undeceived, in the presence of a God who cannot be mocked.

WHEN A MAN SOWS, HE EXPECTS TO REAP.

"Behold, the husbandman waiteth for the precious fruit of the earth, and hath long patience for it, until he receive the early and latter rain."—James v: 7.

CHAPTER III.

When a Man Sows, He Expects to Reap.

Notice these four things about sowing and reaping: A man expects to reap when he sows; he expects to reap the same kind of seed that he sows; he expects to reap more; and ignorance of the kind of seed makes no difference.

First: *When a man sows, he expects to reap.*

If a farmer went on sowing, spring after spring, and never reaping in the autumn, you would say he was a fit subject for the lunatic asylum. No; he is always looking forward to the time when he will reap the reward of his toil. He never expects that the seed he has sown will be lost.

A young man serves a long apprenticeship to some trade or profession; but he expects by and by to reap the fruit of all those years of patient industry. Ask an engineer why he works so hard for five, six, or seven years in the endeavor to learn his profession. He replies that he is looking forward to the reaping time, when his fortune and reputation will be made. The lawyer studies long and hard; but he, too, anticipates the time when his clients will be numerous, and he will be repaid for his toil. A great many medical students have a hard time trying to support themselves while they are at college. As soon as they get their diploma and become doctors they expect that the reaping time is coming; that is what they have been working for.

Some harvests ripen almost immediately, but as a rule we find it true in the natural world that *there is delay* before the seed comes to maturity. It is growing all the time, however; first the little green shoot breaking through the soil, then the blade, then the ear, then the full corn in the ear. The farmer is not disappointed because all his crops do not spring up in a night like mushrooms. He looks forward with patience, knowing that the reaping time will come in due season.

So with the harvest of our actions. Few men, if any, would indulge in sin unless they expected pleasure out of it. A drunkard does not drink for the mere sake of drinking, but in the hope of present enjoyment. A thief does not steal for the mere sake of stealing, but for the sake of gain. And similarly with the good man. He does not make sacrifices merely for the sake of sacrifice, but because thereby he hopes and expects to do good, and help others. All these things are means to ends: there is always expectation of a harvest.

The Certainty of the Reaping.

The text bids us look forward to the certainty of the reaping: "Whatsoever a man soweth, that shall he also reap."

We know what it is to have a failure of the crops, but in the spiritual world no such failure is possible. Wet soil may rot the seed, or frost may nip the early buds, or the weather may prove too wet or too dry to bring the crops to maturity, but none of these things occur to prevent the harvest of one's actions. The Bible tells us that God will render to every man according to his deeds. "To them who by patient continuance in well-doing seek for glory and honor and immortality, eternal life: but unto them that are contentious, and do not obey the truth, but obey unrighteousness, indignation and wrath, tribulation and anguish upon every soul of man that doeth evil." How careful we should be of our actions in all departments of our being, physical, moral, intellectual! The deeds we do, the words we speak, the thoughts we harbor, are all recorded, and shall meet their just reward, for God is no respecter of persons.

And it must not be overlooked that *the harvest comes as a necessary consequence of the sowing*. It has been said that God is not a sort of a moral despot, as He is so frequently regarded. He does not sit on a throne, attaching penalties to particular actions as they come up for judgment. He has laid down certain laws, of which the law of sowing and reaping is one, and punishment is the natural outcome of sin. There is no escape. It must be borne; and though others may have to reap *with* you, no one can reap *for* you.

The text teaches, further, that *the harvest is one or other of two kinds*. There are two, and only two, directions in which the law leads: Sowing to the flesh, and a harvest of corruption—sowing to the Spirit, and a harvest of everlasting life.

Sowing to the Flesh.

"Sowing to the flesh" does not mean simply taking due care of the body. The body was made in the image of God, and the body of a believer is a temple of the Holy Ghost, and we may be sure that due care for the image is well-pleasing to God. The expression refers rather to pandering to the lusts of the body, pampering it, providing gratification for its unlawful desires at the expense of the higher part of a man, indulging the animal propensities which in their excess are sinful. "Sowing to the flesh" is scattering the seeds of selfishness, which always must yield a harvest of corruption.

"When we were in the flesh, the motions of sins did work in our members to bring forth fruit unto death." And what does Paul say are the works of the flesh? "Adultery, fornication, uncleanness, lasciviousness, idolatry, witchcraft, hatred, variance, emulations, wrath, strife, seditions, heresies, envyings, murders, drunkenness, revellings, and such like."

I was at the Paris exhibition in 1867, and I noticed there a little oil painting, only about a foot square, and the face was the most hideous I have ever seen. On the paper attached to the painting were the words "Sowing the tares," and the face looked more like a demon's than a man's. As he sowed these tares, up came serpents and reptiles, and they were crawling up on his body, and all around were woods with wolves and animals prowling in them. I have seen that picture many times since. Ah! the reaping time is coming. If you sow to the flesh you must reap the flesh. If you sow to the wind you must reap the whirlwind.

And yet it must not be thought that indulgence in the grosser vices is the only way of sowing to the flesh. Every desire, every action that has not God for its end and object is seed sown to the flesh. If a man is sowing for a harvest of money or ambition, he is sowing to the flesh, and will reap corruption, just as surely as the liar and adulterer. No matter how "polite" and "refined" and "respectable" the seed may be, no matter how closely it resembles the good seed, its true nature will out, the blight of corruption will be upon it.

How foolish are the strivings of men in view of this judgment! Many a man will sacrifice time, health—even his character—for money. What does he gain? Corruption; something that is not eternal, that has not the qualities of "everlasting life." John said, "The world passeth away, and the lust thereof." Peter said, "All flesh is as grass, and all the glory of man as the flower of grass. The grass withereth, and the flower thereof falleth away." None of these fleshly things have their roots in the eternal. You may even outlive them in your own short life.

No Bridge Between.

Now, men make this mistake—they sow to the flesh, and they think they will reap the harvest of the spirit; and on the other hand, they sow to the spirit and are disappointed when they do not reap a temporal harvest.

A teacher had been relating to his class the parable of the rich man and Lazarus, and he asked:

"Now, which would you rather be, boys, the rich man or Lazarus?"

One boy answered, "I would rather be the rich man while I live, and Lazarus when I die."

That cannot be: it is flesh and corruption, or, Spirit and everlasting life. There is no bridge from one to the other.

"Seed which is sown for a spiritual harvest has no tendency whatever to procure temporal well-being. Christ declared, 'Blessed are the pure in heart; for they shall see God; blessed are they that hunger and thirst after righteousness, for they shall be filled' (with righteousness); 'blessed are they that mourn, for they shall be comforted.' You observe the beatific vision of the Almighty—fulness of righteousness—divine comfort. There is nothing earthly here, it is spiritual results for spiritual labor. It is not said that the

21

pure in heart shall be made rich; or that they who hunger and thirst after righteousness shall be filled with bread, or that they who mourn shall rise in life, and obtain distinction. Each department has its own appropriate harvest, reserved exclusively to its own method of sowing.

"Everything reaps its own harvest, every act has its own reward. And before you covet the enjoyment which another possesses, you must first calculate the cost at which it was procured.

"For instance, the religious tradesman complains that his honesty is a hindrance to his success; that the tide of custom pours into the doors of his less scrupulous neighbor in the same street, while he himself waits for hours idle. My brother, do you think that God is going to reward honor, integrity, high-mindedness, with this world's coin? Do you fancy that He will pay spiritual excellence with plenty of custom? Now consider the price that man has paid for his success. Perhaps mental degradation and inward dishonor. His advertisements are all deceptive, his treatment of his workmen tyrannical, his cheap prices made possible by inferior articles. Sow that man's seed, and you will reap that man's harvest. Cheat, lie, be unscrupulous in your assertions, and custom will come to you. But if the price be too high, let him have his harvest, and you take yours—a clear conscience, a pure mind, rectitude within and without. Will you part with that for his harvest?"

Sowing to the Spirit.

"Sowing to the Spirit" implies self-denial, resistance of evil, obedience to the Spirit, walking in the Spirit, living in the Spirit, guidance by the Spirit. We sow to the Spirit when we use our abilities and means to advance Spiritual things; when we support and encourage those who are extending the influence of the Spirit. We sow to the Spirit when we crucify the flesh and all its lusts, when we yield ourselves to Him as we once yielded ourselves to the flesh. A Jewish rabbi once said: "There are in every man two impulses, good and evil. He who offers God his evil impulses offers the best sacrifice."

The fruit of such sowing is "love, joy, peace, longsuffering, gentleness, goodness, faith, meekness, temperance."

In this world the harvest is growth of character, deeper respect, increasing usefulness to others; in the next world, acceptance with God, everlasting life.

Among the last recorded words of Henry Lloyd Garrison in his public speeches in England were these "I began my advocacy of the anti-slavery cause in the Northern States of America, in the midst of brickbats and rotten eggs; and I ended it on the soil of South Carolina almost literally buried beneath the wreaths of flowers which were heaped upon me by her liberated bondmen."

A young man was employed by a large commission firm in New York City during the late civil war, to negotiate with a certain party for a lot of damaged beans. The beans were purchased, delivered, and spread out upon the upper floor of the building occupied by the firm.

Men were employed to turn them over and over, and to sprinkle them with a solution of soda, so as to improve their appearance and render them more salable. A large lot of the first quality of beans was then purchased; some of the good beans were first put into barrels, then the barrels were nearly filled with the poor ones; after this the good ones were again put on the top and the barrels headed up for sale.

The employer marked the barrels, "Beans—A 1." The clerk seeing this, said: "Do you think, sir, that it is right to mark those beans A 1?"

The employer retorted sharply: "Are you head of the firm?"

The clerk said no more. The barreling and heading went on. When all was ready, the beans (many hundreds of barrels) were put on the market for sale. Specimens of the best quality were shown in the office to buyers.

At length a shrewd purchaser came in (no man is so sharp in business but he will often meet his equal), examined the samples in the office, inquired the price, and then wished to see the stock in bulk. The clerk was ordered to go with the buyer to the upper loft and show him the stock. An open barrel was shown apparently of the same quality of the sample. The buyer then said to the clerk:

"Young man, the samples of beans shown me are of the first quality, and it is impossible to purchase beans anywhere in the market for the price at which you offer them; there is something wrong here. Tell me, are these beans the same quality throughout the entire barrel as they appear on the top?"

The clerk now found himself in a strange position. He thought, "Shall I lie for my employer, as he undoubtedly means I shall; or shall I tell the truth, come what will?" He decided for the truth, and said:

"No, sir, they are not."

"Then," said the customer. "I do not want them"; and he left.

The clerk enterers the office. The employer said to him: "Did you sell that man those beans?"

He said, "No, sir."

"Why not?"

"Well, sir, the man asked me if those beans were of the same quality through the entire barrel as they appeared on the top. I told him they were not. He then said: 'I do not want them,' and left."

"Go to the cashier," said the employer, "and get your wages; we want you no longer."

He received his pay and left the office, rejoicing that he had not lied for the purposes of abetting a sordid avariciousness, and benefiting an unprincipled employer.

Three weeks after this the firm sent after the young clerk, entreated him to come back again into their employ, and offered him three hundred dollars salary more per year than they had ever before given him.

And thus was his honesty and truthfulness rewarded. The firm knew and felt that the man was right, although apparently they had lost largely by his honesty. They wished to have him again in their employ, because they knew that they could trust him, and never suffer through fraud and deception. They knew that their financial interests would be safe in his custody. They respected and honored that young man.

The Lesson of Patience.

Let us learn the lesson of patience. "Behold the husbandman waiteth for the precious fruit of the earth, and hath long patience for it, until he receive the early and latter rain." Delay does not mean denial. Too often one generation sows and another has to reap. God is a jealous God, "visiting the iniquity of the fathers upon the children unto the third and fourth generation of them that hate Him."

In the early years of Israel's existence as a separate people, God commanded them to give the land of Canaan rest every seventh year.

"Six years thou shalt sow thy land, and shalt gather in the fruits thereof: but the seventh year thou shalt let it rest and lie still; that the poor of thy people may eat, and what they leave the beasts of the field shall eat. In like manner thou shalt deal with thy vineyard, and with thy olive yard." From the anointing of Saul to be king this law was not observed. After four hundred and ninety years God gave the nation into captivity for seventy years. During this period the land had rest; seventy sabbath years to compensate for the sabbath years of which it had been deprived. Those Israelites sowed the bitter seed of disobedience, and their descendants had to reap the harvest in exile and captivity.

A leading surgeon performed a critical operation before his class one day. The operation was successful, as far as his part was concerned. But he turned to the class and said: "Six years ago a wise way of living might have prevented this disease. Two years ago a safe and simple operation might have cured it. We have done our best to-day as the case now stands, but Nature will have her word to say. She does not always repeal her capital sentences." Next day the patient died, reaping the fruit of his excesses.

Paul says: "Let us not be weary in well-doing; in due season we shall reap if we faint not."

In a recent chat with an interviewer, Mr. Edison quite unconsciously preached a most powerful sermon on perseverance and patience.

He described his repeated efforts to make the phonograph reproduce the aspirated sound, and added: "From eighteen to twenty hours a day for the last seven months I have worked on this single word 'specia.' I said into the phonograph, 'specia, specia, specia,' but the instrument responded, 'pecia, pecia, pecia.' It was enough to drive one mad! But I held firm, and I have succeeded."

An insurance case was brought to Daniel Webster when he was a young lawyer in Portsmouth. Only a small amount was involved, and a twenty-dollar fee was all that was promised. He saw that to do his client full justice, a journey to Boston would be desirable, in order to consult the law library. He would be out of pocket by the expedition, and for the time he would receive no adequate compensation. But he determined to do his best, cost what it might. He accordingly went to Boston and looked up the authorities, and gained the case.

25

Years after, Webster, who had meanwhile become famous, was passing through New York. An important insurance case was to be tried that day, and one of the counsel had suddenly been taken ill. Money was no object, and Webster was begged to name his terms and conduct the case.

"I told them," said Mr. Webster, "that it was preposterous to expect me to prepare a legal argument at a few hours notice. They insisted, however, that I should look at the papers; and this I finally consented to do. It was my old twenty-dollar case over again; and as I never forget anything, I had all the authorities at my fingers' ends. The court knew that I had no time to prepare, and were astonished at the range of my acquirements. So you see, I was handsomely repaid both in fame and money for that journey to Boston; and the moral is that good work is rewarded in the end."

Two men were digging in California for gold. They worked a good deal and got nothing. At last one of them threw down his tools and said:

"I will leave here before we starve"; and he left.

The next day his comrade's patience was rewarded by finding a nugget that supported him until he made a fortune.

"Because sentence against an evil work is not executed speedily, therefore the heart of the sons of men is fully set in them to do evil. Though a sinner do evil an hundred times, and his days be prolonged, yet surely I know that it shall be well with them that fear God, which fear before Him; but it shall not be well with the wicked, neither shall he prolong his days, which are as a shadow; because he feareth not before God."

The idea that because a person does a thing in the dark it will never be brought to light, is fatal—God says it *shall* be brought to light. It is folly for a man who has covered his sins to think there shall be no resurrection of them and no final adjudication. Look at the sons of Jacob. They sold Joseph and deceived their father. Twenty long years rolled away, and away down to Egypt their sin followed them; for they said: "We are guilty of the blood of our brother." The reaping time had come at last, for those ten boys who sold their brother.

I was once preaching in Chicago, and a woman who was nearly out of her mind came to me. You know there are some people who mock at religions meetings, and say that religion drives people

26

mad. It is *sin* that drives people mad. It is the want of Christ that sinks people into despair. This was the woman's story: She had a family of children. One of her neighbors had died, and her husband had brought home a little child. She said, "I don't want the child," but her husband said, "You must take it and look after it." She said she had enough to do with her own, and she told her husband to take that child away. But he would not. She confessed that she tried to starve the child; but it lingered on. One night it cried all night; I suppose it wanted food. At last she took the clothes and threw them over the child, and smothered it. No one saw her; no one knew anything about it. The child was buried. Years had passed away; and she said, "I hear the voice of that child day and night. It has driven me nearly mad." No one saw the act; but God had seen it, and this retribution followed it. History is full of these things. You need not go to the Bible to find it out.

A MAN EXPECTS TO REAP
THE SAME KIND AS HE SOWS.

"Herb yielding seed after his kind, and the tree yielding fruit . . . after his kind."—Gen. i: 12.

"Do men gather grapes of thorns, or figs of thistles?"—Matt. vii: 16.

"For if ye live after the flesh, ye shall die: but if ye through the Spirit do mortify the deeds of the body, ye shall live."—Romans viii: 13.

CHAPTER IV.

A Man Expects to Reap the Same Kind as He Sows.

If I should tell you that I sowed ten acres of wheat last year and that watermelons came up, or that I sowed cucumbers and gathered turnips, you wouldn't believe it. It is a fixed law that you reap the same kind of seed you sow. Plant wheat and you reap wheat, plant an acorn and there comes up an oak, plant a little elm and in time you have a big elm.

One day, the master of Lukman, an Eastern fabulist, said to him, "Go into such a field, and sow barley." Lukman sowed oats instead. At the time of harvest his master went to the place, and, seeing the green oats springing up, asked him:

"Did I not tell you to sow barley here? Why, then, have you sown oats?"

He answered, "I sowed oats in the hope that barley would grow up."

His master said, "What foolish idea is this? Have you ever heard of the like?"

Lukman replied, "You yourself are constantly sowing in the field of the world the seeds of evil, and yet expect to reap in the resurrection day the fruits of virtue. Therefore I thought, also, I might get barley by sowing oats."

The master was abashed at the reply and set Lukman free.

Like produces like in vegetation, and like produces like in labor. If a man has learnt the trade of a carpenter, he does not expect to excel as a watchmaker. If he has toiled hard to acquire a knowledge of the law, he does not expect to practice medicine for a livelihood. Men expect to reap in the same line as they have learned.

This law is just as true in God's kingdom as in man's kingdom; just as true in the spiritual world as in the natural world. If I sow tares, I am going to reap tares; if I sow a lie, I am going to reap lies; if I sow adultery. I am going to reap adulterers; if I sow whisky, I am going to reap drunkards. You cannot blot this law out, it is in force. No other truth in the Bible is more solemn.

Suppose that a neighbor, whom I don't want to see, comes to my house and I tell my son to tell him, if he asks for me, that I am out of town. He goes to the door and lies to my neighbor; it will not be six months before that boy will lie to me; I will reap that lie.

A man said to me some time ago, "Why is it that we can not get honest clerks now?"

I replied, "I don't know, but perhaps I can imagine a reason. When merchants teach clerks to say that goods are all wool when they are half cotton, and to adulterate groceries and say they are pure, when they grind up white marble and put it into pulverized sugar, and the clerk knows it, you will not have honest clerks."

As long as merchants teach their clerks to lie and to misrepresent, to put a French or an English tag on domestic goods and sell them for imported goods, so long they will have dishonest clerks. Dishonest merchants make dishonest clerks. I am not talking fiction, I am talking truth. It is not poetry, but solemn prose that a man must reap the same kind of seed that he sows.

This is a tremendous argument against selling liquor. Leaving out the temperance and religious aspects of the question, no man on earth can afford to sell strong drink. If I sell liquor to your son and make a drunkard of him, some man will sell liquor to my son and make a drunkard of him. Every man who sells liquor has a drunken son or a drunken brother or some drunken relative. Where are the sons of liquor dealers? To whom are their daughters married? Look around and see if you can find a man who has been in that business twenty years who has not a skeleton in his own family.

I threw that challenge down once, and a man said to me the next day, "I wasn't at your meeting last night, but I understand you made the astounding statement that no man had been in the liquor business twenty years who hadn't the curse in his own family."

"Yes," I said, "I did."

"It isn't true," he said, "and I want you to take it back. My father was a rumseller, and I am a rumseller, and the curse has never come into my father's family or into mine."

I said, "What! two generations selling that infernal stuff, and the curse has never come into the family! I will investigate it, and if I find I am wrong I will make the retraction just as publicly as I did the statement."

There were two prominent citizens of the town in the room, on whose faces I noticed a peculiar expression as the man was talking. After he left, one of them said:

"Do you know, Mr. Moody, that man's own brother was a drunkard and committed suicide a few weeks ago and left a widow with seven children; they are under his roof now! He was a terrible drunkard himself until the shock of his brother's suicide cured him."

I don't know how you can account for it unless he thought his brother wasn't a relative. Perhaps he was a sort of a Cainite, saying, "Am I my brother's keeper?"

When I was a pastor of a church in Chicago we were trying to get hold of the working-men. They used to say:

"Come down to the factory at dinner-time and we will give you a chance to speak."

I would ask them, "Why won't you come to the church?"

"Oh," they would say, "you have it all your own way there, and we can't answer back; but come to the factory and we will put a few questions to you."

So I went down, and they made it pretty hot for me sometimes. One of the favorite characters that they brought up was Jacob. Many a time I have had men say, "You think Jacob was a saint, don't you? He was a big rascal." Many have said they thought Jacob wasn't as good as Esau. Notice this fact. You read in the Bible, "I will punish Jacob according to his doings." This law of retribution runs through his Life; although he was a friend of God, a kinsman of Abraham, and was third in the line of the covenant, yet God made Jacob reap the same kind of seed he sowed. Some one has said that "Jacob's misfortunes were uniformly calculated to bring back to his recollection the picture as well as the punishment of his faults."

When Isaac in his old age wanted some venison, and sent Esau out to get it, Jacob slipped out and took a kid from his father's flock, and Rebekah, his mother, cooked it; he brought it to his old blind father and said he was Esau. The old man recognized his voice, but he had very cunningly put the skin of the kid on his hands and neck; so that the old man felt him and said;

"The voice is Jacob's voice, but the hands are the hands of Esau."

By this lie he got his brother's birthright blessing, but he paid ten thousand times more for it than it was worth. "Who steals my purse steals trash." A man who steals my pocketbook is the chief sufferer, not I. When Jacob had grown to be an old man, he lived in continual suspicion that his sons were deceiving him. The sin of deceiving his own father bore fruit.

Jacob was the great loser in this transaction. When Esau returned he had to flee for his life. Then God met him at Bethel. "And behold, the Lord stood above it and said, I am the Lord God of Abraham thy father, and the God of Isaac: the land whereon thou liest, to thee will I give it, and to thy seed: and thy seed shall be as the dust of the earth: and thou shalt spread abroad to the west and to the east and to the north and to the south, and in thee and in thy seed shall all the families of the earth be blessed.

"And, behold, I am with thee, and will keep thee in all places whither thou goest, and will bring thee again unto this land, for I will not leave thee, until I have done that which I have spoken to thee of."

Men will read that far in the life of Jacob and say, "I don't want anything more to do with a God who will deal in grace with a man who had done so mean a thing." My friend, hold on. Follow him to Padanaram. He was there twenty years, and during that time his wages were changed ten times. He worked seven years for the lovely Rachel, and then had another woman put upon him. Jacob had by deception obtained the blessing of the first-born son, but Laban sarcastically reminded him, "It must not be so done in my country to give the younger before the first-born." He found that Laban could drive as sharp a bargain as he. Wherever you find a sharp, shrewd man, you will always find that he draws just such men around him, and that he who cheats will himself be cheated. "Birds of a feather flock together"; blasphemers get together, and sharp, shrewd men get together. Jacob found in Laban just such a man as himself. It was "diamond cut diamond."

Look a little further. Jacob had twelve sons, but he loved Joseph and Benjamin more than the others because they were the sons of his beloved Rachel. He was partial to Joseph, and had a coat made of many colors for him. Partiality will raise the old Adam in any family.

One morning Joseph, in the innocence of his heart, tells a dream in which his father and all his brothers had bowed down to him. Then his brothers began to plan to get him out of the way, and when his father sent him to find them when they were tending the flocks, they said:

"Now we have him; let us slay him and cast him into a pit, and say that some beast has devoured him."

Later they sold him, and took his coat of many colors and dipped it in the blood of a kid, and, taking it to their father, said: "This have we found; know now whether it be thy son's coat or no." And he knew it and said, "It is my son's coat; an evil beast hath devoured him."

Now notice: Jacob deceived his father with the skin of a kid, and his sons deceived him with the blood of a kid. Jacob lied to his father, and his sons lied to him. The lie came home. Every lie is bound to come back to you. You cannot dig a grave so deep but

31

that it will have a resurrection. Tramp, tramp, your sins will all come back.

"Be sure your sin will find you out." You may think you are very shrewd and far-sighted, and can plan and cover up, but it is the decree of high heaven that no sin shall be covered; God will uncover it. You cannot deceive the Almighty. Jacob found that out. He had to reap what he sowed.

Again, look at David. A man said to me some years ago: "Don't you think David fell as low as Saul?"

Yes, he fell lower, because God had lifted him higher. The difference is that when Saul fell there was no sign of repentance, but when David fell, a wail went up from his broken heart; there was true repentance. No man in all the Scripture record rose so high and fell so low as David. God took him from the sheepfold and placed him on the throne. He gave him riches and lands in abundance. He was on a pinnacle of glory, and was loved and honored among men. But one day, you remember, David was walking upon the roof of the king's house, and he saw Bathsheba, and lusted after her, and committed the awful sin of adultery; and then, to cover up that sin, he made Bathsheba's husband drunk, and had him murdered. The decree came: "I will raise up evil in thy family and the sword shall never leave thy house." Amnon, David's son, commits adultery with David's own daughter. Absalom makes a feast for Amnon and has him murdered. Not long after he comes with an army to drive David, his father, from the throne, and publicly commits adultery with David's concubines on the roof of the king's house; if God had not been overruling, he would have killed his father.

David sowed adultery and reaped it in his own family. He sowed murder and reaped it in his own family. I believe that what brought the bitter wail from that father's heart when he said, "Oh, my son Absalom, my son, my son Absalom! Would God I had died for thee," was the fact that these were the wages of his own sin. From the time he fell into that sin with Uriah's wife until he went down to his grave, it was one billow after another rolling over him.

If God did not spare David, do you think He will spare us if we fall into sin and do not confess and turn from our sins? If ever a man had an opportunity to cover his sins, David had. No judge or jury dared to pronounce judgment against him. The thing was done

32

in the dark, but his sin found him out. Nathan was sent across his path, and, young man, Nathan will appear to you some day. Some messenger will smite you in the way if you do not repent and turn from your sins. My friend, why not call on God now as David did when he came to himself? make the same prayer—how thankful we should be that we have the prayer! why not make it on your knees now?

David's Prayer for Forgiveness.

"Have mercy upon me, O God, according to thy loving kindness: according unto the multitude of thy tender mercies blot out my transgressions.

Wash me thoroughly from mine iniquity, and cleanse me from my sin. For I acknowledge my transgressions; and my sin is ever before me.

Against thee, thee only, have I sinned, and done this evil in thy sight; that thou mightest be justified when thou speakest, and be clear when thou judgest.

Behold, I was shapen in iniquity; and in sin did my mother conceive me.

Behold, thou desirest truth in the inward parts; and in the hidden part thou shalt make me to know wisdom.

Purge me with hyssop, and I shall be clean; wash me, and I shall be whiter than snow.

Make me to hear joy and gladness; that the bones which thou hast broken may rejoice.

Hide thy face from my sins, and blot out all mine iniquities.

Create in me a clean heart, O God, and renew a right spirit within me.

Cast me not away from thy presence; and take not thy Holy Spirit from me.

Restore unto me the joy of thy salvation; and uphold me with thy free Spirit.

Then will I teach transgressors thy ways; and sinners shall be converted unto thee.

Deliver me from bloodguiltiness, O God, thou God of my salvation; and my tongue shall sing aloud of thy righteousness.

O Lord, open thou my lips; and my mouth shall shew forth thy praise.

For thou desirest not sacrifice; else would I give it; thou delightest not in burnt offering. The sacrifices of God are a broken spirit: a broken and a contrite heart, O God, thou wilt not despise."

Examples From History.

But you say you don't believe in the Bible. Then look at history, and see if this law is not true. Maxentine built a false bridge to drown Constantine, but was drowned himself. Bajazet was carried about by Tamerlane in an iron cage which he intended for Tamerlane. Maximinus put out the eyes of thousands of Christians; soon after a fearful disease of the eyes broke out among his people, of which he himself died in great agony. Valens caused about eighty Christians to be sent to sea in a ship and burnt alive: he was defeated by the Goths and fled to a cottage, where he was burnt alive.

Alexander VI. was poisoned by wine he had prepared for another. Henry III. of France was stabbed in the same chamber where he had helped to contrive the cruel massacre of French Protestants. Marie Antoinette, riding to Notre Dame Cathedral for her bridal, bade the soldiers command all beggars, cripples, and ragged people to leave the line of the procession. She could not endure the sight of these miserable ones. Soon after, bound in the executioner's cart, she was riding toward the place of execution amidst crowds who gazed on her with hearts as cold as ice and hard as granite. When Foulon was asked how the starving populace was to live, he said: "Let them eat grass." Afterward, the mob, maddened with rage, caught him in the streets of Paris, hung him, stuck his head upon a pike and filled his mouth with grass.

A MAN REAPS MORE THAN HE SOWS.

"But other fell into good ground, and brought forth fruit, some a hundredfold, some sixtyfold, some thirtyfold."—Matt. xiii: 8.

CHAPTER V.

A Man Reaps More Than He Sows.

If I sow a bushel, I expect to reap ten or twenty bushels. I can sow in one day what will take ten men to reap. The Spaniards have this proverb: "Sow a thought and reap an act. Sow an act, and reap a habit. Sow a habit, and reap a character. Sow a character and reap a destiny." *And it takes a longer time to reap than to sow.* I have

34

heard of a certain kind of bean that reproduces itself a thousand fold. One thistle-down which blew from the deck of a vessel is said to have covered with thistles the entire surface of a South Sea island. The oak springs from an acorn, the mighty Mississippi from a little spring.

One glass of whisky may lead to a drunkard's death. One lie may ruin a man's career. One error in youth may follow a man all through life. Some one has said that many a Christian spends half his time trying to keep down the sprouts of seed sown in his young days. Unless it is held in check, the desire to "have a drink" will become a consuming thirst; the desire to "play a game of cards" an irresistible gambler's passion.

Abraham gave up his only son at God's bidding, and as the fruit of that act of obedience God gave him seed as numerous as the stars of the heaven and as the sands upon the seashore.

Jacob told one lie, and his ten sons came back with his lie multiplied tenfold. For twenty years Jacob mourned for Joseph, supposing that he was dead. I have no doubt that night after night he wept for Joseph, and in his dreams saw the boy torn to pieces, and heard his cries for help. It took him a long time to reap the harvest.

Israel murmured against God because of the report of the land of Canaan brought back by the spies. Had they not to reap a multiplied harvest? Listen: "After the number of the days in which ye searched the land, even forty days, each day for a year, shall ye bear your iniquities, even forty years, and ye shall know my breach of promise."

When I made the remark in a meeting once that a man had to reap more than he sowed, a man in front of me dropped his head and sobbed aloud. After the meeting, a friend stepped up to him and said:

"What is your trouble?"

Pointing to me he said, "Every word that man has been saying is true. Four years ago I was the confidential clerk of a firm in this city. I have reason to believe that if I had continued as I began, I should have been in the firm now. But one night in a saloon under the influence of drink I committed a crime, and I was sent to the penitentiary, where I repented in sackcloth and ashes. To-day I came back for the first time, and went to the old house, and they ordered me out. I went to other business-houses I was acquainted with, and received the same treatment. I met men on the street whom I once knew, who had held inferior places to me, and I lifted my hat, but no one returned the bow."

The man wrung his hands in agony and said, "It is all true, it takes a longer time to reap than to sow."

Do you not believe it? Ask your neighbor who has drank up his character and reputation and home, and has brought a blight on his family. It takes a long time to build up a character, but you can blast it in a single hour.

A man died in the Columbus penitentiary some years ago who had spent over thirty years in his cell. He was one of the millionaires of Ohio. Fifty years ago when they were trying to get a trunk road from Chicago to New York, they wanted to lay the line through his farm near Cleveland. He did not want his farm divided by the railroad, so the case went into court, where commissioners were appointed to pay the damages and to allow the road to be built. One dark night after the tracks were laid, a train was thrown off the track, and several were killed. This man was suspected, was tried and found guilty, and was sent to the penitentiary for life. The farm was soon cut up into city lots, and the man became a millionaire, but he got no benefit from it. Before he died, the chaplain told me that he became a child of God. It may not have taken him more than an hour to lay the obstruction on the railroad, but he was over thirty years reaping the result of that one act!

In the history of France we read that a certain king wanted some new instrument to torture his prisoners with. One of his favorites suggested that he should build a cage, not long enough to lie down in, and not high enough to stand up in. The king accepted the suggestion; but the first one put into the cage was the very man who suggested it, and he was kept in it for fourteen years. It did not take him more than a few minutes, perhaps, to suggest that cruel device; but he was fourteen long years reaping the fruit of what he had sown.

If a man could do his reaping alone, it would not be so hard; but it is terrible when he has to make that godly father, and that mother who loves him, or that wife and family, reap along with him. Does not the drunkard make his wife and children reap a bitter harvest?

Does not the gambler make his relatives reap? Does not the harlot make her parents reap agony and shame? What a bitter enemy is sin! May God help each one of us to turn from it at once!

Whenever I hear a young man talking in a flippant way about sowing his wild oats, I don't laugh. I feel more like crying, because I know he is going to make his gray-haired mother reap in tears; he is going to make his wife reap in shame; he is going to make his old father and his innocent children reap with him. Only ten or fifteen or twenty years will pass before he will have to reap his wild oats; no man has ever sowed them without having to reap them. Sow the wind and you reap the whirlwind.

We cannot control our influence. If I plant thistles in my field, the wind will take the thistle-down when it is ready, and blow it away beyond the fence; and my neighbors will have to reap with me. So my example may be copied by my children or my neighbors, and my actions reproduced indefinitely through them, whether for good or evil. How many have gone to ruin because of the sins of such men as Jacob and David and Lot!

Nothing But Leaves.

Nothing but leaves! The Spirit grieves
O'er years of wasted life!
O'er sins indulged while conscience slept,
O'er vows and promises unkept,
And reap from years of strife—
Nothing but leaves! Nothing but leaves!
Nothing but leaves! No gathered sheaves
Of life's fair ripening grain;
We sow our seeds; lo! tares and weeds—
Words, *idle* words, for earnest deeds—
Then reap, with toil and pain,
Nothing but leaves! Nothing but leaves!
Nothing but leaves! Sad memory weaves
No veil to hide the past;
And as we trace our weary way,
And count each lost and misspent day,
We sadly find at last—
Nothing but leaves! Nothing but leaves!
Ah, who shall thus the Master meet,
And bring but withered leaves?
Ah, who shall, at the Saviour's feet,

Before the awful judgment-seat,
Lay down, for golden sheaves,
Nothing but leaves! Nothing but leaves?
—L. E. Ackerman.

IGNORANCE OF THE SEED MAKES NO DIFFERENCE.

"Marvel not at this: for the hour is coming, in the which all that are in the graves shall hear his voice, and shall come forth, they that have done good; unto the resurrection of life; and they that have done evil, unto the resurrection of damnation."—John v: 28, 29.

CHAPTER VI.

Ignorance of the Seed Makes no Difference.

Now, notice again: Ignorance of the kind of seed makes no difference. If I think I am sowing good seed and it happens to be bad, I shall have a bad harvest; therefore, it becomes me to see what kind of seed I am sowing.

Suppose I meet a man who is sowing seed, and say: "Hello, stranger, what are you sowing?"

"Seed."

"What kind of seed?"

"I don't know."

"Don't you know whether it is good or bad?"

"No, I can't tell; but it is seed, that is all I want to know, and I am sowing it."

You would say that he was a first-class lunatic, wouldn't you? But he wouldn't be half so mad as the man who goes on sowing for time and eternity, and never asks himself what he is sowing or what the harvest will be.

Father, what seed are you sowing in your family? Are you setting your children a good or a bad example? Do you spend your time at the saloon or the club, until you have become almost a stranger to them? or are you training them for God and righteousness?

The story is told that a man once said he would not talk to his son about religion; the boy should make his own choice when he grew up, unprejudiced by him. The boy broke his arm, and when the doctor was setting it, he cursed and swore the whole time.

"Ah," said the doctor, "you were afraid to prejudice the boy in the right way, but the devil had no such prejudice. He has led your son the other way." The idea that a father is to let his children run wild! Nature alone never brings forth anything but weeds.

One of Coleridge's friends once objected to prejudicing the minds of the young by selecting the things they should be taught. The philosopher-poet invited him to take a look at his garden, and took him to where a luxuriant growth of ugly and infragrant weeds spread themselves over beds and walks alike.

"You don't call that a garden!" said his friend.

"What!" said Coleridge, "would you have me prejudice the ground in favor of roses and lilies?"

Have you never noticed the same thing about the mind and the heart? Let a child be idle, and Satan will soon lead him into mischief. He must be looked after. Those things that will help to develop character must be selected for him, and hurtful things must be kept out, just as industriously as the farmer cultivates the useful products of the soil, but wages continual war on weeds and all unwholesome growths.

A murderer was to suffer the penalty of his crime. Speaking of his reckless career, he said:

"How could it be otherwise, when I had such bad training? I was taught these things from my youth. When only four years old my mother poured whisky down my throat to see how I would act."

On the morning of his execution, the wretched mother bade good-bye to the son whom her influence had helped to that shameful end.

A father started for his office early one morning, after a light fall of snow. Turning, he saw his two year-old boy endeavoring to put his tiny feet in his own great footprints. The little fellow shouted: "Go on, I'se comin', papa, I'se comin' right in ure tracks."

He caught the boy in his arms and carried him to his mother, and started again for his office.

His habit had been to stop on the way at a saloon for a glass of liquor. As he stood upon the threshold that morning he seemed to hear a sweet voice say: "Go on, I'se comin', papa, I'se comin' right in ure tracks."

He stopped, he hesitated, he looked the future squarely in the face.

"I cannot afford to make any tracks I would be ashamed or sorry to have my boy walk in," he said decidedly, and turned away.

Father, mother, neighbor, are your tracks true? Are they straight? Can you turn to any walking behind you and say: "Follow me as I follow Christ?" Are you leading the little ones safe to the Great Shepherd?

The best time to sow the good seed is before Satan has scattered the tares. God has given numerous warnings and instructions to do it. "Seek ye *first* the Kingdom of God and his righteousness." "Train up a child in the way he should go." "Provoke not your children to wrath, but bring them up in the nurture and admonition of the Lord." If a farmer neglects to plant in the spring-time, he can never recover the lost opportunity: no more can you, if you neglect yours. Youth is a seed-time, and if it is allowed to pass without good seed being sowed, weeds will spring up and choke the soil. It will take bitter toil to uproot them.

An old divine said that when a good farmer sees a weed in his field he has it pulled up. If it is taken early enough, the blank is soon filled in, and the crop waves over the whole field. But if allowed to run too late, the bald patch remains. It would have been better if the weed had never been allowed to get root.

Young man, are you letting some secret sin get the mastery over you, binding you hand and foot? It is growing. Every sin grows. When I was speaking to five thousand children in Glasgow some years ago, I took a spool of thread and said to one of the largest boys:

"Do you believe I can bind you with that thread?"

He laughed at the idea. I wound the thread around him a few times, and he broke it with a single jerk. Then I wound the thread around and around, and by and by I said:

"Now get free if you can."

He couldn't move hand or foot. If you are slave to some vile habit, you must either slay that habit or it will slay you.

My friend, *what kind of seed are you sowing?* Let your mind sweep over your record for the past year. Have you been living a double life? Have you been making a profession without possessing what you profess? If there is anything you detest it is hypocrisy. Do you tell me God doesn't detest it also? If it is a right eye that offends, make up your mind that you will pluck it out; or

40

if it is a right hand or a right foot, cut it off. Whatever the sin is, make up your mind that you will gain the victory over it without further delay.

What kind of seed are you sowing, my friend, good seed or bad seed? There will be a harvest, and you are bound to reap, whether you want to or not. Tell me, how do you spend your spare time? Telling vile stories, polluting the minds of others, while your own mind is also polluted? Do you read any literature that makes your thoughts impure? How do you spend the Sabbath? Boating, fishing, hunting, or on excursions? Do you think ministers are old fogies—that the Bible belongs to the dark ages? Tell me bow you treat your parents, and I will tell you how your children will treat you. A man was making preparations to send his old father to the poorhouse, when his little child came up and said:

"Papa, when you are old shall I have to take you to the poorhouse?"

Do you never write home to your parents? They clothed you and educated you, and now do you spend your nights in gambling? You say to your godless companions that your father crammed religion down your throat when you were a boy. I have a great contempt for a man who says that of his father or mother. They may have made a mistake; but it was of the head, not of the heart. If a telegram was sent to them that you were down with smallpox, they would take the first train to come to you. They would willingly take the disease into their own bodies and die for you. If you scoff and sneer at your father and mother you will have a hard harvest; you will reap in agony. It is only a question of time. There is a saying—

"The mills of God grind slowly,
But they grind exceeding small."

The Lord Jesus said, "With what measure ye mete, it shall be measured to you again."

A man told me when I was last in London that England had the advantage of America in one respect. I asked how. He said:

"We have more respect for our laws in England than you do in America. You don't hang half your murderers, but all our murderers are hanged if they can be proved guilty."

I said: "Neither country hangs its worst murderers. If my son wants to murder me, I would rather have him kill me outright than

41

to take five years to do it. A young man who goes home late night after night, and when his mother remonstrates, curses her gray hairs, and kills her by inches, is the worst sort of a murderer."

That is being done all over the country. You may not be guilty of a sin as black and as foul as this, but I tell you, every sin grows, and if you have sin in your heart you cannot tell where it will land you. Nothing separates a son from his mother or a man from his wife like sin. The grace of God binds men together, but sin tears them apart and separates them.

Come, my friend, what kind of seed are you sowing? What will the harvest be? Will it be a black harvest, or are you going to have a joyful harvest? If you think that, when you have sown tares, wheat will come up, you are greatly mistaken. If you think you can give a loose rein to your passions and lusts, and yet have eternal life, you are being deceived. For God says, "He that soweth to his flesh shall of the flesh reap corruption; but he that soweth to the Spirit shall of the Spirit reap life everlasting."

Choose Carefully.

I beg of you to *choose carefully your path.* The farmer is careful in the choice of seed. He does not want bad seed or inferior seed, because he knows that such will give a poor crop. He looks for the best seed he can buy. If you choose to sow to the flesh, you will have a corrupted harvest. If you commit a sinful deed, it may land you into a dishonored grave.

Choice is a solemn thing. You can make this moment a turning-point in your life. Once during the conquest of Peru, Pizzaro's followers threatened to desert him. They gathered on the shore to embark for home. Drawing his sword, he traced a line with it in the sand from east to west. Then turning toward the south he said:

"Friends and comrades, on that side are toil, hunger, nakedness, the drenching storm, and death; on this side, ease and pleasure. There lies Peru with all its riches; here Panama and its poverty. Choose each man as becomes a brave Castilian. For my part, I go south."

So saying, he stepped across the line, and one after another his comrades followed him, and the destiny of South America was decided.

Napoleon was once offered a position as officer in the Turkish artillery. He declined it; but had he chosen to accept it, the history of Europe would have been different.

On your choice in spiritual things depends your eternity. On the one side there is Christ; on the other, the world. Between them you must choose. Do not wish to grow both wheat and tares. Oh, choose Christ! Let there be no half-heartedness. Give Him your whole heart. He died to redeem you from the curse of sin, and He lives to save you from the power of sin.

"No man can serve two masters." You can not belong to two kingdoms at once. Lord Brougham grew to be so fond of Cannes that he sought to be naturalized as a Frenchman, but found it was impossible to be both a peer of England and a citizen of a French town; he must renounce the one to become the other.

Now this is where *the will* comes in It is easy to follow other people's lead, to swim with the tide; but it requires character, moral back-bone, to stand against the current of popular opinion and practice. During the late war a deserter came into the Federal lines before Pittsburg. He was asked:

"What did you go into secession for?"

His answer was: "Because they all did."

That reason will account for many a man's action. He will act according to the saying: "While you are in Rome, do as the Romans do," neglecting to investigate and determine whether or not the Romans do right. If they do wrong, a man should stand against a whole nation, if need be, like another Daniel.

Almighty God set two sides before the children of Israel, and I set them now before you. Remember, as you choose, that your eternity is in the balance.

"See, I have set before thee this day life and good, and death and evil; in that I command thee this day to love the Lord thy God, to walk in His ways, and to keep His commandments, and His statutes, and His judgments, that thou mayest live and multiply; and the Lord thy God shall bless thee in the land whither thou goest to possess it.

But if thine heart turn away, so that thou wilt not hear, but shalt be drawn away, and worship other gods, and serve them: I denounce unto you this day that ye shall surely perish, and that ye shall not prolong your days upon the land whither thou passest over Jordan to go to possess it.

I call heaven and earth to record this day against you, that I have set before you life and death, blessing and cursing: therefore CHOOSE LIFE that both thou and thy seed may live: that thou mayest love the Lord thy God, and that thou mayest obey His voice, and that thou mayest cleave unto Him: for He is thy life and the length of thy days."

FORGIVENESS AND RETRIBUTION.

"Thou renderest to every man according to his work."—Psalms lxii: 12.

"For we must all appear before the judgment seat of Christ; that every one may receive the things done in his body, according to that he hath done, whether it be good or bad."—II Cor. v: 10.

CHAPTER VII.

Forgiveness and Retribution.

I can imagine some one saying, "I attend church, and have heard that if we confess our sin, God will forgive us; now I hear that I must reap the same kind of seed that I have sown. How can I harmonize the doctrine of forgiveness with the doctrine of retribution? 'All we like sheep have gone astray; we have turned every one to his own way; and the Lord hath laid on him the iniquity of us all.' And yet you say that I must reap what I have sown."

Suppose I send my hired man to sow wheat. When it grows up, there are thistles mixed with the wheat. There wasn't a thistle a year ago. I say to my man:

"Do you know anything about the thistles in the field?"

He says: "Yes, I do; you sent me to sow that wheat, and I was angry and mixed some thistles with the wheat. But you promised me that if I ever did wrong and confessed it, you would forgive me; now I hold you to that promise, and expect you to forgive me."

"Yes," I say, "you are quite right; I forgive you for sowing the thistles; but I will tell you what you must do—you must reap the thistles along with the wheat when harvest time comes."

Many a Christian man is reaping thistles with his wheat. Twenty years ago you sowed thistles with the wheat and are reaping them now. Perhaps it was an obscene story, the memory of which keeps coming back to distress you, even at the most solemn moments. Perhaps some hasty word or deed that you have never been able to recall.

I heard John B. Gough say that he would rather cut off his hand than have committed a certain sin. He didn't say what it was, but I have always supposed it was the way he treated his mother. He was a wretched, drunken sot in the gutter when his mother died; the poor woman couldn't stand it, and died of a broken heart. God had forgiven him, but he never forgave himself. A great many have done things that they will never forgive themselves for to their dying day. "At this moment," said one, "from many a harlot's dishonored grave there arises a mute appeal for righteous retribution. From many a drunkard's miserable home, from heartbroken wife, from starving children, there rings up a terrible appeal into the ears of God."

I believe that God forgives sin fully and freely for Christ's sake; but He allows certain penalties to remain. If a man has wasted years in riotous living, he can never hope to live them over again. If he has violated his conscience, the scars will remain through life. If he has soiled his reputation, the effect of it can never be washed away. If he shatters his body through indulgence and vice, he must suffer until death. As Talmage says, "The grace of God gives a new heart, but not a new body."

"John," said a father to his son, "I wish you would get me the hammer."

"Yes, sir."

"Now a nail and a piece of pine board."

"Here they are, sir."

"Will you drive the nail into the board?"

It was done.

"Please pull it out again."

"That's easy, sir."

"Now, John," and the father's voice dropped to a lower key, "pull out the nail hole."

Every wrong act leaves a scar. Even if the board be a living tree the scar remains.

For our worst sins there is plenteous redemption. My sin may become white as snow, and pass away altogether, in so far as it has power to disturb or sadden my relation to God. Yet our least sins leave in our lives, in our characters, in our memories, in our consciences, sometimes in our weakness, often in our worldly position, in our reputation, in our success, in our health, in a thousand ways leave their traces and consequences. God will not put out His little finger to remove these, but lets them stop.

Let no man fancy that the Gospel which proclaims forgiveness can be vulgarized into a mere proclamation of impunity. Not so. It was to *Christian men* that Paul said, 'Be not deceived, God is not mocked: whatsoever a man soweth, that shall he also reap.' God loves us too well not to punish His children when they sin, and He loves us too well to annihilate (were it possible) the *secondary* consequences of our transgressions. The two sides of the truth must be recognized—that the deeper and (as we call them) the *primary* penalties of our evil, which are separation from God and the painful consciousness of guilt, are swept away; and also that other results are allowed to remain, which, being allowed, may be blessed and salutary for the transgressors.

MacLaren says, "If you waste your youth, no repentance will send the shadow back upon the dial, or recover the ground lost by idleness, or restore the constitution shattered by dissipation, or give back the resources wasted upon vice, or bring back the fleeting opportunities. The wounds can all be healed, for the Good Physician, blessed be His name! has lancets and bandages, and balm and anodynes for the deadliest; but scars remain even when the gash is closed."

God forgave Moses and Aaron for their sins, but both suffered the penalty. Neither one was permitted to enter the promised land. Jacob became a "prince of God" at the ford of Jabbok, but to the end of his days he carried in his body the mark of the struggle. Paul's thorn in the flesh was not removed, even after most earnest and repeated prayer. It lost its sting, however, and became a means of grace.

Perhaps that is one reason why God does not remove these penalties of sin. He may intend them to be used as tokens of His chastening. "Whom the Lord loveth He chasteneth." And if the temporal consequences were completely removed we would be liable to fall back again into sin. The penalty is a continual reminder of our weakness, and of the need of caution and dependence upon God.

One night in Chicago at the close of a meeting in the Y. M. C. A. rooms, a young man sprang to his feet and said: "Mr. Moody, would you let me speak a few words?"

I said, "Certainly."

Then for about five minutes he pleaded with those men to break from sin. He said:

"If you have anyone who takes any interest in your spiritual welfare, treat them kindly, for they are the best friends you have. I was an only child, and my mother and father took great interest in me. Every morning at the family altar father used to pray for me, and every night he would commend me to God. I was wild and reckless and didn't like the restraint of home. When my father died my mother took up the family worship. Many a time she came to me and said, Oh, my boy, if you would stay to family worship I should be the happiest mother on earth; but when I pray, you don't even stay in the house. Sometimes I would go in at midnight from a night of dissipation and hear my mother praying for me. Sometimes in the small hours of morning I heard her voice pleading for me. At last I felt that I must either become a Christian or leave home, and one day I gathered a few things together and stole away from home without letting my mother know.

"Some time after I heard indirectly that my mother was ill. Ah, I thought, it is my conduct that is making her ill! My first impulse was to go home and cheer her last days; but the thought came that if I did I should have to become a Christian. My proud heart revolted and I said: 'No, I will not become a Christian.'"

Months rolled by, and at last he heard again that his mother was worse. Then he thought:

"If my mother should not live I would never forgive myself."

That thought took him home. He reached the old village about dark, and started on foot for the home, which was about a mile and a half distant. On the way he passed the graveyard, and thought he would go to his father's grave to see if there was a newly-made grave beside it. As he drew near the spot, his heart began to beat faster, and when he came near enough, the light of the moon shone on a newly-made grave. With a great deal of emotion he said:

"Young men, for the first time in my life this question came over me—who is going to pray for my lost soul now? Father is gone, and mother is gone, and they are the only two who ever cared for me. If I could have called my mother back that night and heard her breathe my name in prayer, I would have given the world if it had been mine to give. I spent all that night by her grave, and God for Christ's sake heard my mother's prayers, and I became a child ot God. But I never forgave myself for the way I treated my mother, and never will."

Where is my wandering boy to-night-——
The boy of my tenderest care,
The boy that was once my joy and light.
The child of my love and prayer?
Once he was pure as morning dew,
As he knelt at his mother's knee;
No face was so bright, no heart more true,
And none was so sweet as he.
O, could I see you now, my boy,
As fair as in olden time,
When prattle and smile made home a joy,
And life was a merry chime.
Go for my wandering boy to-night,
Go, search for him where you will;
But bring him to me with all his blight,
And tell him I love him still.

My dear friends, God may forgive you, but the consequences of your sin are going to be bitter even if you are forgiven.

A few years ago I was preaching in Chicago on that text, "Arise, go up to Bethel and dwell there." After the meeting a man asked to see me alone. I went into a private room. The perspiration stood in beads on his forehead. I said:

"What is it?"

He replied: "I am a fugitive from justice. I am in exile, in disguise. The government of my state has offered a reward for me. I have been hidden here for months. They tell me there is no hell, but it seems as though I have been in hell for months."

He had been a business man, and having, as he thought, plenty of money, he forged some bonds, thinking that he could give his check any time and call them in, but he got beyond his depth and fell.

He said, "I have been here for six months. I have a wife and three children, but I cannot write to them or hear from them." The poor man was in terrible mental agony.

I said, "Why don't you go back and give yourself up and face the law, and ask God to forgive you?"

He said, "I would take the first train to-morrow and give myself up, except for one thing. I have a wife and three children; how can I bring the disgrace upon them?"

I, too, have a wife and three children, and when he said that, the thing looked very different.

Ah! if we could do our own reaping, it would not be so bitter, but when we make our little children or the wife of our bosom, or our old gray-haired mother, or our old father reap with us, isn't the reaping pretty bitter? I don't fear any pestilence or any disease as much as I fear sin. If God will only keep sin out of thy family, I will praise Him in time and in eternity. The worst enemy that ever crossed a man's path is sin.

If a man comes to me for advice I always try to put myself in the place of the one to whom I am talking, and then to give the best advice I can. I said to this man,

"I don't know what to say, but it is safe to pray."

After I had prayed, I urged him to pray; but he said:

"If I do, it means the penitentiary."

I asked him to come the next day at twelve. He met me at the appointed hour, and said:

"It is all settled; if I ever meet the God of Bethel I must go through the prison to meet Him, and God helping me, I will give myself up. I am going back, and I should like to have you keep quiet until I give myself over into the hands of the law; then you may hold me up as a warning. Little did I think when I started out in life that I was coming to this! Little did I think when I married a girl from one of the first families in the state that I should bring such disgrace on her."

At four o'clock that afternoon he went back to Missouri. He reached home a little past midnight, and spent a week with his family. In a letter he said that he didn't dare let his children know he was there, lest they should tell the neighbor's children. At night he would creep out and look at his children, but he couldn't take

49

them in his arms or kiss them. Oh, there is the result of sin! Would to God we could every one of us just turn from sin to-day!

One day, when this man was in hiding, he heard his little boy say: "Mamma, doesn't papa love us any more?"

"Yes," his mother replied. "Why do you ask?" "Why," the little fellow said, "he has been gone so long and he never writes us any letters and never comes to see us."

The last night he came out from hiding and took a long look at those innocent, sleeping children; then he took his wife and kissed her again and again, and leaving that once happy home he gave himself up to the sheriff. The next morning he pleaded guilty, and was sent to the penitentiary for nineteen years. I believe that God had forgiven him, but he couldn't forgive himself, and he had to reap what he sowed. I pleaded with the governor for mercy, and the man was pardoned.

Some time ago I was telling this story, and some one doubted it, but the governor who pardoned him happened to be in the meeting, and rose and said, "I pardoned that man myself." The governor pardoned him, and he lived a few years, but from the time he committed that sin he had to reap. Oh, reader, I plead with you, overcome your besetting sin, whatever it is.

Future Punishment.

I can imagine some one saying, "I am glad Mr. Moody hasn't tried to scare us about the future state. I agree with him that we shall receive all our reward and punishment in this life."

If you think I believe that, you are greatly mistaken. One sentence from the lips of the Son of God in regard to the future state has forever settled it in my mind. "*If ye die in your sins, where I am, there ye cannot go.*" If a man has not given up his drunkenness, his profanity, his licentiousness, his covetousness, heaven would be hell to him. Heaven is a prepared place for prepared people. What would a man do in heaven who cannot bear to be in the society of the pure and holy down here?

It is not true that all reward and punishment is reaped in this life. Look how many crimes are committed, and the perpetrators are never caught. It often happens that the worst criminal uses his experience to escape detection, while a more innocent hand is captured. A man ruins a girl. Does he always reap punishment here? No. He holds his head as high as ever in society, while the unfortunate victim of his lust, who, perhaps, was innocently beguiled into sin by him, becomes an outcast. His punishment, however is, at the latest, only adjourned to another world.

Eternity!

Oh, the clanging bells of Time!
Night and day they never cease;
We are wearied with their chime,
For they do not bring us peace.
And we hush our breath to hear,
And we strain our eyes to see
If thy shores are drawing near—
Eternity! Eternity!
Oh, the clanging bells of Time!
How their changes rise and fall,
But in undertone sublime,
Sounding clearly through them all,
Is a voice that must be heard,
As our moments onward flee,
And it speaketh aye one word—
Eternity! Eternity!
Oh, the clanging bells of Time!
To their voices loud and low,
In a long, unresting line
We are marching to and fro;
And we yearn for sight or sound,
Of the life that is to be,
For thy breath doth wrap us round—
Eternity! Eternity!
Oh, the clanging bells of Time!
Soon their notes will all be dumb,
And in joy and peace sublime
We shall feel the silence come;
And our souls their thirst will slake,
And our eyes the King will see,
When thy glorious morn shall break—
Eternity! Eternity!
—Ellen M. H. Gates

WARNING.

"Take heed that no man deceive you."—Matt. xxiv: 4.

"Christ in you, the hope of glory, whom we preach, warning every man, and teaching every man in all wisdom; that we may present every man perfect in Christ Jesus."—Col. i: 27, 28.

CHAPTER VIII.

WARNING.

To give a warning is a sign of love. Who warns like a mother, and who loves like a mother? Your mother, perhaps, is gone, and your father is gone. Let me take the place of those who have departed, and lift up a warning voice. With Paul I would say: "I write not these things to shame you, but as my beloved sons I warn you."

A pilot guiding a steamer down the Cumberland saw a light, apparently from a small craft, in the middle of the narrow channel. His impulse was to disregard the signal and run down the boat. As he came near, a voice shouted: "Keep off, keep off."

In great anger he cursed what he supposed to be a boatman in his way. On arriving at his next landing he learned that a huge rock had fallen from the mountain into the bed of the stream, and that a signal was placed there to warn the coming boats of the unknown danger. Alas! many regard God's warnings in the same way, and are angry with any who tell them of the rocks in their course. They will understand better at the end.

The children of Israel had no truer friend than Moses. They never went astray but he warned them; and trouble never came upon them except when his warnings were unheeded. Elijah was the best friend Ahab had.

I wish I could warn as Jesus Christ did. As he went up Mount Olivet, His heart seemed to be greatly moved and He cried, "Oh, Jerusalem, Jerusalem, thou that killest the prophets, and stonest them which are sent unto thee, how often would I have gathered thy children together, even as a hen gathereth her chickens under her wings, and ye would not!" Did He not warn?

If a friend of mine were about to invest in a worthless silver-mine, do you think I would be true to him if I did not caution him against it? And do I show less love for him because I warn him against actions that will bring a harvest of misery and despair?

"Whosoever heareth the sound of the trumpet, and taketh not warning; if the sword come, and take him away, his blood shall be upon his own head; he heard the sound of the trumpet, and took not warning; his blood shall be upon him. But he that taketh warning shall deliver his soul."

Be sure that the seed you are sowing is good seed. Sow to the flesh, and a good harvest will be impossible. Good seed and bad seed cannot both succeed if allowed to grow together. One prospers at the expense of the other; and the likelihood is that the bad will get the upper hand. Weeds always seem to grow and spread more rapidly than good seed.

The longer they live, the firmer hold the weeds are gaining. Delay is dangerous. In the year 1691, a proclamation was sent through the Highlands of Scotland, that every one who had been guilty of rebellion against the constituted government would be pardoned, if, before the last day of the year, he laid down his arms and promised to cease his rebellion. Many did so; but one chief named Maclan put off submission from week to week, always intending to submit before it was too late. But when, at last, he started to accept pardon, he was hindered by a great storm and did not arrive until the time had expired. The day of pardon had passed and the day of vengeance had come; Maclan and his men were put to death.

Hence, it is wise to exterminate the weeds at once. And beware of remaining longer in sin. The deeper you sink, the more bitter will be your restoration. Why continue to sear you conscience, and sow the seeds of keener remorse? No matter how painful it may be, break with sin at once. Severe operations are often necessary, for the skilful surgeon knows that the disease cannot be cured by surface applications. The farmer takes his hoe and his spade and his axe, and he cuts away the obnoxious growths, and burns the roots out of the ground with fire.

If thy right eye offend thee, pluck it out, and cast it from thee: for it is profitable for thee that one of thy members should perish, and not that thy whole body should be cast into hell. And if thy right hand offend thee, cut it off, and cast it from thee: for it is profitable for thee that one of thy members should perish, and not that thy whole body should be cast into hell.

Remember that the tares and the wheat will be separated at the judgment day, if not before. Sowing to the flesh and sowing to the spirit inevitably lead in diverging paths. The axe will be laid at the root of the trees, and every tree that bringeth not forth good fruit will be hewn down and cast into the fire. The threshing-floor will be thoroughly purged, and the wheat will be gathered into the garner, while the chaff will be burned with unquenchable fire.

Beware of your habits. A recent writer has said: "Could the young but realize how soon they will become mere walking bundles of habits, they would give more heed to their conduct while in the plastic state. We are spinning our own fates, good or evil, and never to be undone. Every smallest stroke of virtue or of vice leaves its never so little scar. The drunken Rip Van Winkle, in Jefferson's play, excuses himself for every fresh dereliction by saying, '*I won't count this time.*' Well, he may not count it, and a kind heaven may not count it, but it is being counted none the less. Down among his nerve cells and fibres the molecules are counting it, registering and storing it up, to be used against him when the next temptation comes. Nothing we ever do is, in strict scientific literalness, wiped out. Of course, this has its good side as well as its bad one. As we become permanent drunkards by so many separate drinks, so we become saints in the moral sphere, and authorities and experts in the practical and scientific spheres, by so many separate acts and hours of work."

Beware of temptations. "Lead us not into temptation," our Lord taught us to pray: and again he said, "Watch and pray, lest ye enter into temptation." We are weak and sinful by nature, and it is a good deal better for us to pray for deliverance rather than for strength to resist when temptation has overtaken us. Prevention is better than cure. Hidden under the soil may be seeds of passion and wickedness that only wait for a favorable opportunity to shoot up.

Young men pretend that it is necessary to see both sides of life. What foolishness! I am not called upon to put my hand in the fire to see if it will burn.

A steamboat was stranded on the Mississippi river, and the captain could not get her off. Eventually a hard-looking fellow came on board and said:

"Captain, I understand you want a pilot to take you out of this difficulty?"

The captain said, "Are you a pilot?"

"Well, they call me one."

"Do you know where the snags and sand-bars are?"

"No sir,"

"Well, how do you expect to take me out of here if you don't know where the snags and sand-bars are?"

"I know where they ain't!" was the reply.

Begin to sow the good seed while the children are young, and thus prevent the weeds getting a start. Satan does not wait till they grow up, and no more should we.

There are many fishing nets so constructed as to allow none but full grown fish to be caught, the immature escaping. Satan has none such. He catches the weakest and youngest.

"We must care for our boys or the devil will," said a young Sabbath School teacher.

"The devil will care for them anyway," answered the old superintendent: "The devil will not neglect them even though we do."

It is a master-piece of the devil to make us believe that children can not understand religion. Would Christ have made a child the standard of faith if He had known that it was not capable of understanding His words? It is far easier for children to love and trust than for grown-up persons, and so we should set Christ before them as the supreme object of their choice.

Do not neglect opportunities. Napoleon used to say: "There is a crisis in every battle—ten or fifteen minutes—on which the issue of the battle depends. To gain this is victory; to lose it is defeat."

Beware of sin. Its wages are Death, and (as has been said) the wages have never been reduced. It deceives men as to the satisfaction to be found in it, the excuses to be made for it, and the certainty of the punishment that must follow. If it was not deceitful, it would never be delightful. It comes in innocent guise, and saps the life blood, depriving one of the moral capacity to do good. Canon Wilberforce walking in the Isle of Skye, saw a magnificent eagle soaring upward. He halted and watched its flight. Soon he observed something was wrong. It began to fall, and presently lay dead at his feet. Eager to know the reason of its death, he examined it and found no trace of gunshot wound; but he saw in its talons a small weazel, which, in its flight, drawn near its body, had sucked the life blood from the eagle's-breast. Such is the end of every one who persistently clings to sin.

Do not be deceived by the attractiveness of this world. It will cheat you and destroy you. "The Redoubtable" was the name of a

French ship that Lord Nelson spared twice from destruction; and it was from the rigging of that very ship that the fatal ball that killed him was fired. The devil administers many a sin in honey; but there is poison mixed with it. The truest pleasures spring from the good seed of righteousness—none else are profitable.

Beware of ignorance and indifference. You cannot afford to neglect your soul. There is too much at stake. I never knew an idle man to be converted. Until he wakes up and realizes his lost and hopeless condition, God Almighty will not reach down and take him by the hand. A ship was once in great danger at sea, and all but one man were on their knees. They called to him to come and join them in prayer, but he replied:

"Not I; it's your business to look after the ship. I'm only a passenger."

Remember that mere knowledge is not enough. Many a man knows the gospel precepts and promises by heart who is not touched by saving grace. Knowledge is often useless or positively harmful, and what we want is to know God's will and observe it. Even good resolutions are not enough. No doubt they are helpful in their way, but the Bible does not lead us to believe that they can save a man. It does not say: "As many as *resolved to receive* Him, to them gave He power to become the sons of God, even to them that *resolve to believe* on His name"; it says: "As many as *received* Him * * * *believe* on His name."

Be watchful! There is constant need to be on guard lest we fall into sin. "Set a double guard upon that point to-night," was the command of a prudent officer when an attack was expected. At the best there will be some tares among the wheat. We, all of us, carry around with us material that Satan can work on. Paul said:

"For I know that in me (that is, in my flesh) dwelleth no good thing: for to will is present with me; but how to perform that which is good I find not. For the good that I would, I do not: but the evil which I would not, that I do. Now if I do that I would not, it is no more I that do it, but sin that dwelleth in me. I find then a law, that, when I would do good, evil is present with me. For I delight in the law of God after the inward man: but I see another law in my members, warring against the law of my mind, and bringing me into captivity to the law of sin which is in my members. O wretched man that I am! who shall deliver me from the body of this death?"

Blessed be God, he could add: "I thank God through Jesus Christ our Lord."

The issue that God has placed before us is clear-cut: "He that believeth on the Son hath everlasting life; and he that believeth not the Son shall not see life; but the wrath of God abideth on him." There is no middle course—"he that believeth"—"he that believeth not." He leaves us to choose, and the responsibility rests upon ourselves.

It may cost you many a sacrifice, and wrench many a heart-string to choose aright, but I plead with you to take the decisive step now. The salvation of your soul outweighs all other considerations. Will you imperil your eternity for the sake of some present gain or pleasure? Bow your head and say: "Heavenly Father, I now choose to come unto Thee as a poor, suppliant sinner. I believe on Thy Son, whom Thou didst send to be my Savior; and trusting in the merits of His blood, which was shed as a propitiation for my sins, I rest in the assurance of sins forgiven."

There is hope for the vilest sinner. Wherever weeds grow, there is the possibility of good seed growing. The greater your need, the more welcome will you be to Jesus. The proud and the self-confident He knoweth afar off, but the faintest whisper of the contrite sinner commands His attention.

Our Lord gave us a simple test to help us in our choice. He said, "Every tree is known by its fruit. A good tree bringeth not forth corrupt fruit, neither doth a corrupt tree bring forth good fruit." Many of us have not the time or ability to unravel intricate arguments, or grasp profound doctrines. Certain phases of truth are often inaccessible to the ordinary mind. But the test Christ gave is short and practical, and within the reach of any one of us.

"Have you ever heard the gospel?" asked a missionary of a Chinaman, whom he had not seen in his mission before.

"No," he replied, "but I have seen it. I know a man who used to be the terror of his neighborhood. He was a bad opium smoker and dangerous as a wild beast; but he became wholly changed. He is now gentle and good and has left off opium."

Apply this test to infidelity. What are its fruits? Crime follows in its track. Society becomes disorganized. Chastity, honesty and the other virtues are undermined. The whole life is blighted.

The following brief extract from a letter written in an english prison, is a tremendous arraignment of that system of belief which does not acknowledge God:

"I am one of thirteen infidels. Where are my friends? Four have been hanged. One became a Christian. Six have been sentenced to various terms of imprisonment, and one is now confined in a cell just over my head, sentenced to imprisonment for life."

With all reverence we may apply this text to our Lord Himself. We have His own authority for it. On one occasion when the jews cavilled at His actions, He said: "The works which the Father hath given me to finish, the same works that I do, bear witness of me, that the Father hath sent me." On another occasion they gathered round Him and asked, "How long dost thou hold us in suspense? If thou be the Christ, tell us plainly." Jesus answered: "I told you, and ye believed not. The works that I do in my Father's name, they bear witness of me. * * * If I do not the works of my Father, believe me not. But if I do, though you believe not me, believe the works: that ye may know and believe that the Father is in me, and I in Him." Well might the ruler Nicodemus say, "Rabbi, we know that thou art a teacher come from God: for no man can do these miracles that thou doest, except God be with him." And Peter: "Ye men of Israel, hear these words: Jesus of Nazareth, a man approved of God among you by miracles and wonders and signs, which God did by Him in the midst of you, as ye yourselves know."

What are the fruits of extravagance, of pride, of covetousness? And on the other hand, of prayer, of fearing God and doing His commandments? What are the fruits of heathenism? Look at Africa and China and India and the islands of the seas with their gods of wood and stone. What must be the intelligence and moral sense of people who will worship such things?

Even the best of non-Christian religions must always prove a failure. It cannot be denied that many of the highest virtues are enjoined in the writings of heathen philosophers. How could it be otherwise? Morality is universal as humanity, and it is only to be expected that here and there some thinker should pierce beyond the average and read deeper into the foundation-truths of ethics. This fact only proves, in my mind, the intimate connection between the human and the divine. Christianity never claimed to introduce a brand-new system of morality.

Referring to another matter, Christ said: "Think not that I am come to destroy the law and the prophets: I am not come to destroy, but to fulfill." And so the fulness and perfection of His own system could not fail to embrace many principles that had already appeared in heathen morality. But in the hands of our Savior they became broader and brighter and fuller of power and meaning.

Will these non-Christian religions bear the test? Stoicism was perhaps the noblest of the Greek philosophies, but it rapidly developed into utter cynicism, and culminated in the asserted impossibility of attaining to virtue. Epicureanism started out fairly well, but its founder was not dead before it earned for itself the opprobrious epithet that it was a doctrine worthy only of swine. Look at Buddhism, with its filthy ceremonies and cruel tortures. All these systems exhibit a conflict between theory and practice. They failed in their object, because they approached the difficulty on the wrong side. They trimmed away at the branch, not recognizing that the tree was rotten at heart.

Christianity alone will stand the test of raising man out of the pit. And how does it propose to do it? Not by minimizing the danger and need. It says: "The whole head is sick, and the whole heart faint. From the sole of the foot even unto the head there is no soundness in it; but wounds and bruises and putrefying sores." It demands as *the first necessity* a new birth, regeneration by the Holy Spirit. "Ye must be born again." It does not place sanctification before justification, but having first imparted life from above, it throws around the redeemed sinner the love of Christ and the fellowship and guidance of the Holy Spirit.

A converted Chinaman once said: "I was down in a deep pit, half sunk in the mire, crying for some one to help me out. As I looked up I saw a venerable, grayhaired man looking down at me.

"'My son,' he said, 'this is a dreadful place.'

'Yes,' I answered, 'I fell into it; can't you help me out?'

'My son,' was his reply, 'I am Confucius. If you had read my books and followed what they taught, you would never have been here.'

'Yes, father,' I said, 'but can't you help me out?'

As I looked he was gone. Soon I saw another form approaching, and another man bent over me, this time with closed eyes and folded arms. He seemed to be looking to some far-off place.

'My son,' Buddha said, 'just close your eyes and fold your arms, and forget all about yourself. Get into a state of rest. Don't think about anything that can disturb. Get so still that nothing can move you. Then, my child, you will be in such delicious rest as I am.'

'Yes, father,' I answered, 'I will when I am above ground. Can't you help me out?' But Buddha, too, was gone.

I was just beginning to sink into despair when I saw another figure above me, different from the others. There were marks of suffering on His face. I cried out to Him:

'O, Father! can you help me?'

'My child,' He said, 'what is the matter?'

Before I could answer Him, He was down in the mire by my side. He folded His arms about me and lifted me up; then He fed me and rested me. When I was well He did not say: Now, don't do that again, but He said: 'We will walk on together now'; and we have been walking together until this day."

This was a poor Chinaman's way of telling of the compassionate love and help of the Lord Jesus.

I was reading, some time ago, of a young man who had just come out of a saloon, and had mounted his horse. As a certain deacon passed on his way to church, he followed and said,

"Deacon, can you tell me how far it is to hell?"

The deacon's heart was pained to think that a young man like that should talk so lightly; he passed on and said nothing. When he came round the corner to the church, he found that the horse had thrown that young man, and he was dead. So you may be nearer the Judgment than you think.

When I was in Switzerland many years ago, I learned some solemn lessons about the suddenness with which death may overtake us. I saw several places where land-slides had occurred, completely destroying whole villages; or where avalanches had swept down the mountain sides, leaving destruction in their wake. A terrible calamity happened in the year 1806 to a village, called Goldau, situated in a fertile valley at the foot of the Rossberg mountain. The season had been unusually wet, and this had made the crops all the more abundant.

Early one morning a young peasant, passing the cottage of an old man whom he knew, saw him sitting at the door in the full rays of the sun.

"Good morning, neighbor," said he; "we are likely to have a fine day."

"Time we should have a fine day," growled the old man; "it has been wet enough lately."

"Have you heard the report?" said the other. "Those who were up the earliest this morning declare they saw the top of old Rossberg move."

"Indeed! like enough," said the old man. "Mark my words, and I have often said it before; I shan't live to see it, but those who are now young will not live to be as old as I am before the top of yonder mountain lies at its foot."

"I hope it will not be in my day," said the young man; and he passed on, little thinking how near the prediction was to a fulfilment, and that the ripening fields of corn and the abundant clusters of luscious grapes would never be gathered; but so it was.

The springs of water in the mountain had been overcharged by the excessive rains, and these, in forcing their way to the surface and toward the valley below, had loosened the masses of rounded rock which had been cemented together by a kind of clay, of which material the upper part of the mountain was formed. These huge masses at length gave way and fell headlong into the valley, burying the entire village and about eight hundred of its inhabitants beneath their weight.

But what became of the old man? Alas! he did not escape. He believed the mountain would fall, but he did not think the fall was so near. He was sitting in his cottage, composedly smoking his pipe, when the young man came hastily back, and crying out:

"The mountain is falling!"

The old man composedly rose from his seat, looked out at his door, and saying:

"I shall have time to fill my pipe again," went back into his house.

The young man was saved. The old man perished before he had left his cottage, it and its owner were crushed, and swept to the bottom of the valley.

I was in the north of England, in 1881, when a fearful storm swept over that part of the country. A friend of mine, who was a minister at Eyemouth, had a great many of the fishermen of the place in his congregation. It had been very stormy weather, and the fishermen had been detained in the harbor for a week. One day, however, the sun shone out in a clear blue sky; it seemed as if the storm had passed away, and the boats started out for the fishing-ground. Forty-one boats left the harbor that day. Before they started, the harbor-master hoisted the storm signal, and warned them of the coming tempest. He begged of them not to go; but they disregarded his warning, and away they went. They saw no sign of the coming storm. In a few hours, however, it swept down on that coast, and very few of those fishermen returned. There were five or six men in each boat, and nearly all were lost in that dreadful gale. In the church of which my friend was pastor, I believe there were three male members left.

Those men were ushered into eternity because they did not give heed to the warning. I lift up the storm-signal now, and warn you to escape from the coming judgment!

There was a man living near one of the great trunk roads a number of years ago, who one night saw that a landside had obstructed the track. He saw by the clock that he hadn't time to reach the telegraph office to stop the night express, so he caught up a lantern and started up the track, thinking he might be in time to stop the train. As he ran he fell and put out his light. He hadn't another match, and he could hear the train coming in the distance. He didn't know what to do. As a last resort he stood on the bank, and the moment the train come abreast of him he hurled the lantern with all his might at the engineer. The engineer saw that something must be wrong, took the warning, whistled down the brakes, and stopped the train within a few yards of the obstruction.

I throw the broken lantern at your feet now! I beg you to take warning, make a clear work of sin, cost what it may. Take warning! You must either give up sin, or give up the hope of heaven. Put yourself in the way of being blessed. Make up your mind now that by the grace of God you will obtain the mastery.

"Let the wicked forsake his way, and the unrighteous man his thoughts: and let him return unto the Lord, and He will have mercy upon him; and to our God, for he will abundantly pardon."

Made in the USA
Lexington, KY
12 September 2014